ENOUGH OF YOUR NONSENSE

ENOUGH OF YOUR NONSENSE

GUY JAMES WHITWORTH

with a foreword by Gordon Thompson

CLOUDS OF MAGELLAN PRESS | MELBOURNE

© 2021 Copyright Guy James Whitworth

ISBN: (paperback) 978-0-9874037-9-7

www.guyjameswhitworth.com

Published by Clouds of Magellan Press, Melbourne
www.cloudsofmagellanpress.net

Print and distribution through eBook Alchemy.
www.ebookalchemy.com

Cover and all artwork: Guy James Whitworth

CONTENTS

FOREWORD

This past weekend I walked into a Harvey Norman store and was confronted by a picture of a giant kingfisher – a big, big image in the furnishings section. This was just days after our Prime Minister spoke about asking God for a sign during the 2019 election campaign, then minutes later walking into a gallery and seeing a large picture of a soaring eagle. It showed Mr Morrison that he should, in the words of Isaiah, rise up on eagle's wings.

I was equally inspired by my kingfisher, and straightaway sent a photo to Guy James Whitworth, saying that, just seeing it, I now felt that I was truly doing God's work. Guy, whip smart as usual, shot back a text: 'Yes, but remember, it's only truly god's work if you are jailing families unnecessarily, waving coal around, and misunderstanding the basic concept of sexual assault …'

The text from Isaiah is, for all that, very inspiring – renewing your strength, running and not growing weary – and used to great effect in the film *Chariots of Fire*. You may also recall the actor Ian Charleson's improvised sermon in the same film: 'Where do we find the strength to go on? Jesus said the Kingdom of God is within …' These lines of hope spoken by a gay man.

Guy is a gay man whose words also challenge us to dive deeply into the question of where and how we find the strength to go on; and whose images can make us rise up on the wings of eagles. *The Ascension of Non-Cis Jesus* (p 99) is worth a look in this regard.

Guy and I both come from the north of England and sometimes greet each other with, 'Ha'away, canny lad'. Guy is the quintessential canny lad. He hits the mark, he's funny, he's engaged, irreverent, queer as a kingfisher, and ready to roll in glitter at the drop of a hat. Or hit reply with a smart, insightful text. I hope you enjoy this second book of words and images by Guy.

Gordon Thompson – Clouds of Magellan Press

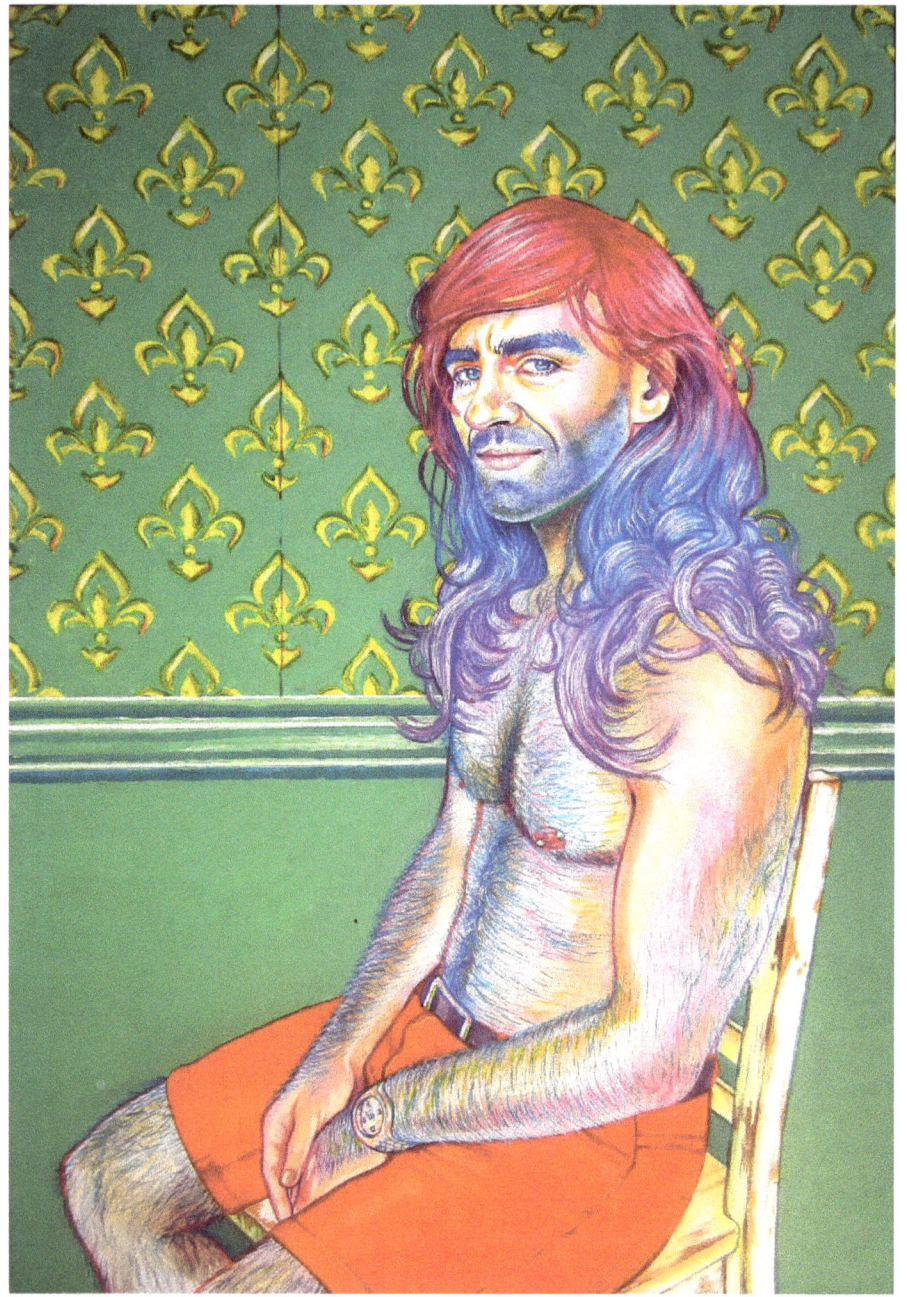

INTRODUCTION
JAMES WITH
THE GOOD HAIR

Probably the worst opening line you could ever read is the author declaring, 'You know, I've never really aspired to be a writer!' But it's true. I always wanted to be an artist. However, more and more people kept asking me about my artworks and the stories behind them, and like most artists nowadays in a time of social media and multiple online platforms, being able to communicate what my work is about, and what I am trying to say with my art practice, is crucial to building up a 'presence' or 'following'.

Two years ago I wrote a book called *Signs of a struggle*, which achieved two things: firstly, it introduced a whole new audience to my work; and secondly, penning it rewired my brain slightly and I started to become slightly and pleasantly 'addicted' to writing.

I have always used my paintings to process and portray what is important to me, and teaching myself to do that through the written word seemed to make just as much sense as painting. More and more now, I find myself sitting at the laptop, on my desk in my studio, rather than standing at a canvas on my easel.

Which, just in case you were wondering, is kinder on the knees, but not kinder to the back.

Like most artists, there are complex reasons why I create, and in no way is any chapter in this book meant as a definitive 'this is why' on any of these paintings. But as I sit and contemplate the whys, the hows and what-fors of each piece, I often realise there is more to what I do than I initially understood.

Last year I was offered a dream job of having a fortnightly column at an online publication called the *Sydney Sentinel*. Luckily for me the editor is a very easy-going and rather open-minded individual and kindly let me write, mostly, about whatever I wanted (and I even got paid for it! Talk about living the dream!). Looking back on my early writings for the *Sydney Sentinel*, well, I think it's fair to say I've progressed with each column, and I think my writing gets better and more accomplished the more I work on it, which is, as I happens, exactly the same as in my art practise.

Also, it's fun now when people ask me what I do, I can make endless double-entendres around the words, 'Oh, I must show you my column!'

This is the first time I have ever written an introduction to a book. I hope it makes clear what this book will be about; basically, I did some pictures and now, using clever sounding words (well to me anyway) funny stories and probably oversharing way too much personal information about myself, explain to you what they are kind of, roughly, mostly about. Most of the works here are taken from my recent exhibition *Enough of your nonsense* (which was a title I came up with, just really so I could print a flyer with the words ENOUGH OF YOUR NONSENSE GUY JAMES WHITWORTH in block capitals, because to be honest, I thought, well everyone is thinking it!).

The painting alongside this introduction is a few years old, but it still is one of my favourite pieces. It is a portrait of my friend James, and no that isn't his real hair although I bet he wishes it was. Obviously it's a wig. Like me, he's a natural tut-tut-baldy-nut. It won the Obi Art Prize a few years ago. The painting, that is, not the hairpiece.

When the organisers called to say I had won the prize, I was walking home from work and at first, I didn't believe that the call was real and I thought it was a friend winding me up. I literally told the woman who had called me to share the good news, (obviously on speaker phone with other people present with her) to go fuck herself and kept asking 'who is this really?' before she convinced me the call was real!

Slightly embarrassing.

Later, on that very same walk home, after the call had ended and I was left grinning like a fool, I walked past a Women's Health Clinic where there was a group of several people demonstrating outside. There was a woman standing holding a placard, and I kid you fucking not, on the placard it said 'All life is sacred' and she was holding this sign WHILE SHE WAS EATING A BURGER. How could anyone in all seriousness hold up the words 'All life is sacred' whilst ramming the flesh of another sentient being down their neck?

Now, come on, surely this ethical dumbfuckery is as exasperating to others as it is to me?

I was so ecstatically happy about winning the Art Prize I initially walked past this hideous group, including the woman greedily gobbling down her own hypocrisy, but I just couldn't do it. I had to go back and tell her, and the other demonstrators what I thought. Anyway, to cut a long story short I ended up screaming in the street at these protestors like I was totally bonkers, and they were the totally sane ones!

Not my proudest moment

Yes, my politics are left of centre and yes, I am very pro-choice. However, I tend not to get too vocal in that opinion because I think it should solely be women that get to decide and discuss women's issues. I mean really, as a gay man, should this be a discussion I am even involved in? Surely the last thing we need in the world is another man spouting opinions about women's bodies, although it is worth pointing out that easily two thirds of the demonstrators outside the clinic were male.

I won't go into details about what I said, or what I called them, because it certainly wasn't anyone's finest moment, but my point being, however, that every time I see this painting, (I don't own it anymore) either on my social media or looking at it in photographs to write about it, like now, I can't help but feel a low-lying sneaky shame at that day when I ended up shouting in the street.

Such are the complexities of art (and also making a public spectacle of oneself).

I will end this introduction with this thought, just in case I forget to say it further on. I want to encourage you, dear reader, to consider and maybe even embark on your own creative journey. Please do not feel restricted by the structure (or limits or failings) of my creative endeavours or voyage, but do, at some point, throughout the reading of this book, please consider your own. Whatever this book makes you feel, if it encourages you to paint, draw, write, collage, doodle, or create in any way you wish, and if that is an outcome, then it will definitely be something I am very proud of.

Guy James Whitworth
May 2021

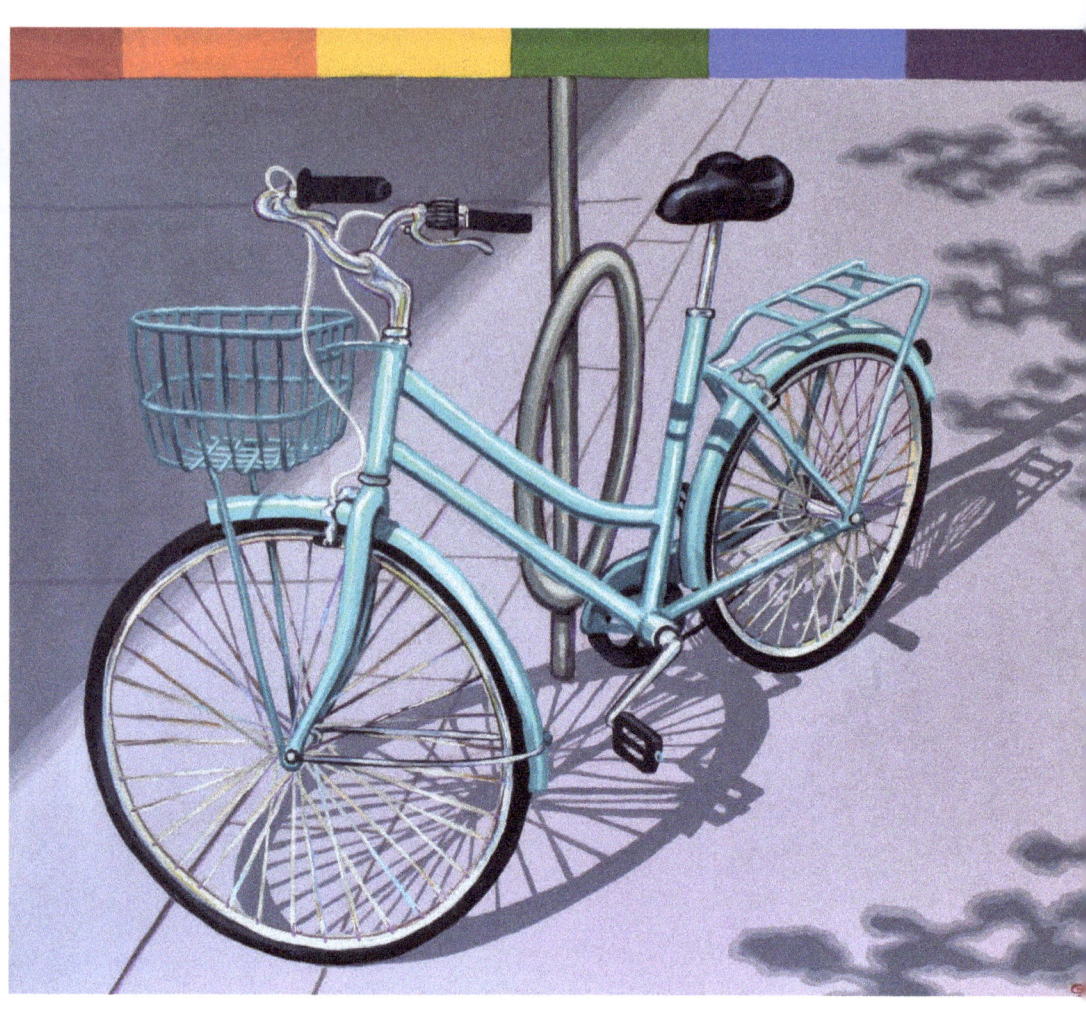

LONELY LIKE RINGWAY PRIMARY SCHOOL

In my work I deal a lot with the concept and emotional outcomes of isolation. Most of the bikes I paint are standing alone in their landscape. They are temporarily an integral part of that landscape yet are never bound by it, or unable to leave.

In fact, the bikes are always unlocked, readily available for adventure! Incidentally, I have always loved the spooky idea of a painting that moves; like if one day a figure is in a certain window in a painting of a house, and then another day they reappear in another window—but now with a blood stain on their clothing. Or a portrait where a sinister beast appears slowly out of the shadows behind the main subject over time. Fuck yeah, I live for that kind of shit. Has that been in a movie? I feel like it has. If not, then I dibs copyright! Anyway, I digress. Isolation is a big, front and centre, aspect of these works. It's an unpredictable wild beast that appears and disappears at will, I am very familiar with.

Between the ages of 5 and 9 I used to go to a school called Ringway Primary School. As photos from the time prove, I was a ridiculously cute child, short and skinny with big soft eyes and a thick shock of unruly dark brown hair. Ringway was about a ten-minute walk from where my family lived, and usually one of my three older sisters would drop me off on their way to a 'bigger' school. My sisters were all popular and pretty girls and as a family we were well known and liked in our local community.

So far so idyllic, yeah?

Well, as we know, slowly over time a scary beast could be appearing.

I was always, as far back as I can remember, artistic and creatively minded. I was always in my own little head a little more than other children. Looking back, I now see that I actually saw the world quite differently from everyone else, even at such an early age. I was never really shy, in the typical meaning of the word shy; but I was always afraid to relax and let my private thought processes or unedited actions out. I was awkwardly guarded and anxious, but yet also randomly flamboyant and erratic. At family get togethers I'd rarely speak, if at all, for fear of 'giving myself away'. I don't doubt these traits must have manifested into me being a rather intense and oddly peculiar child.

When other children were dropped off at Ringway they would usually run up the long pathway that led to the main building and cheerfully hang out in one of the four large playgrounds divided by age. Occasionally children would hang back on the pathway waiting for their friends to arrive.

Obviously, my memories are a tad blurry and approximate from this early age, but I have a clear recollection of feeling like I didn't fit in with the other children and them not wanting to be my friend. I have a very definite memory of hanging out with a couple of other children on a local playing field after school and one of them turning to me and saying the words, 'Learn when you are not wanted!'

Heartbreaking? Yup, just a smidge. Beastly loneliness and bothersome bullies are really what make up the main memories of this time.

By the last few years of that particular school I'd worked out that rather than being in the allocated playground for my age group, I had less chance of being the target of bullies if I stood out on the pathway leading up to the school building looking as if I was waiting for a friend. So I did that most days. The reality, and even at a young age I was aware of this, was that there was no friend to wait for.

Relief would come when the nine o'clock bell would ring, summoning all the children to morning assembly before classes, and I would breathe a sigh of relief that I had managed to avoid either some abuse, harassment or name calling that morning. Play times were also usually spent alone and staying out the way of other children.

As I progressed through the educational system in the North East of England my popularity didn't increase, unfortunately, the bullying did, but I'll get to that later.

I'm now a member of a Facebook group made up of the, now adult, children I went to school with. I stay very quiet in the group and I rarely comment or interact. I do get quite triggered when people say things like 'they were the best years of our lives' when talking about their time at school, but you know, I bite my quick and vicious tongue and I let them have their rosy reminiscences. I mean really, it's an unfair fight if I'm challenging someone on how utterly shit their life must have been since those days spent in a miserable school system in a rainy, economically depressed part of the world. I mean if that was the highlight of everything that they have ever experienced, then yup, I'll bite back anything I have to say. You know the expression 'revenge is a dish best served cold'? Well I never signed on to do the catering and I don't owe anybody anything to chew on. I'll just keep quiet. The best revenge is living well.

My latest exhibition 'Enough of your nonsense' was extended by two weeks. Look, I'm going to say it was extended by popular demand, and that is actually mostly true, (to be honest, it was also because the person who'd booked the gallery after me postponed their show because of economic downturn around COVID-19). But my point is, that now, all grown up and a full planet and half a century away from Ringway Primary School, I'm now really quite popular! Yay for me! I had a booking system for the gallery and people could log in and choose a time and day to come to the gallery and it made me very happy to log on most days and see the names of friends and supporters stack up. Literally those fuckers couldn't get enough of me, some people even came more than once, although that might have been for the gallery wine.

I wish I could walk up that pathway to Ringway Primary school, look that lonely little boy in the eye and tell him he's right to wait, because all the amazing friends he's waiting for, are definitely on their way.

People, and I mean real, grown up lovely people, are now actually drawn to me and like my art, my intensity, randomness and my quirky set of ism's that masquerade as my personality. I am still odd as all fuck, still awkwardly shy with unpredictable flamboyant outbursts, but I think I've kind of learnt to make it work for me. I'll still always be, in my head, the most unpopular kid in the school; but that kind of serves a purpose. It keeps me appreciative of my friends and keeps me humble.

So I guess what I'm saying is, I'm fine with isolation when it happens. I've tamed and trained that scary beast, I've made it my productive, almost cuddly pet. I'm fine with unpopularity, whenever that comes to visit, and I'm also fine with my own company. And I'm really lucky because I get to work through these things in my art practice, and other people relate to my art because òf that! Things that I don't put time into processing are bitterness and resentment, because really, why the fuck would I? Most awesome people have had to face unpopularity and isolation at some point. What doesn't kill you makes you stronger and a much better fuck, or whatever that expression is.

Thank you to all those children that didn't want to be my friend as a child, you created a person that I like, other people want to spend time with and I think that is a very good thing.

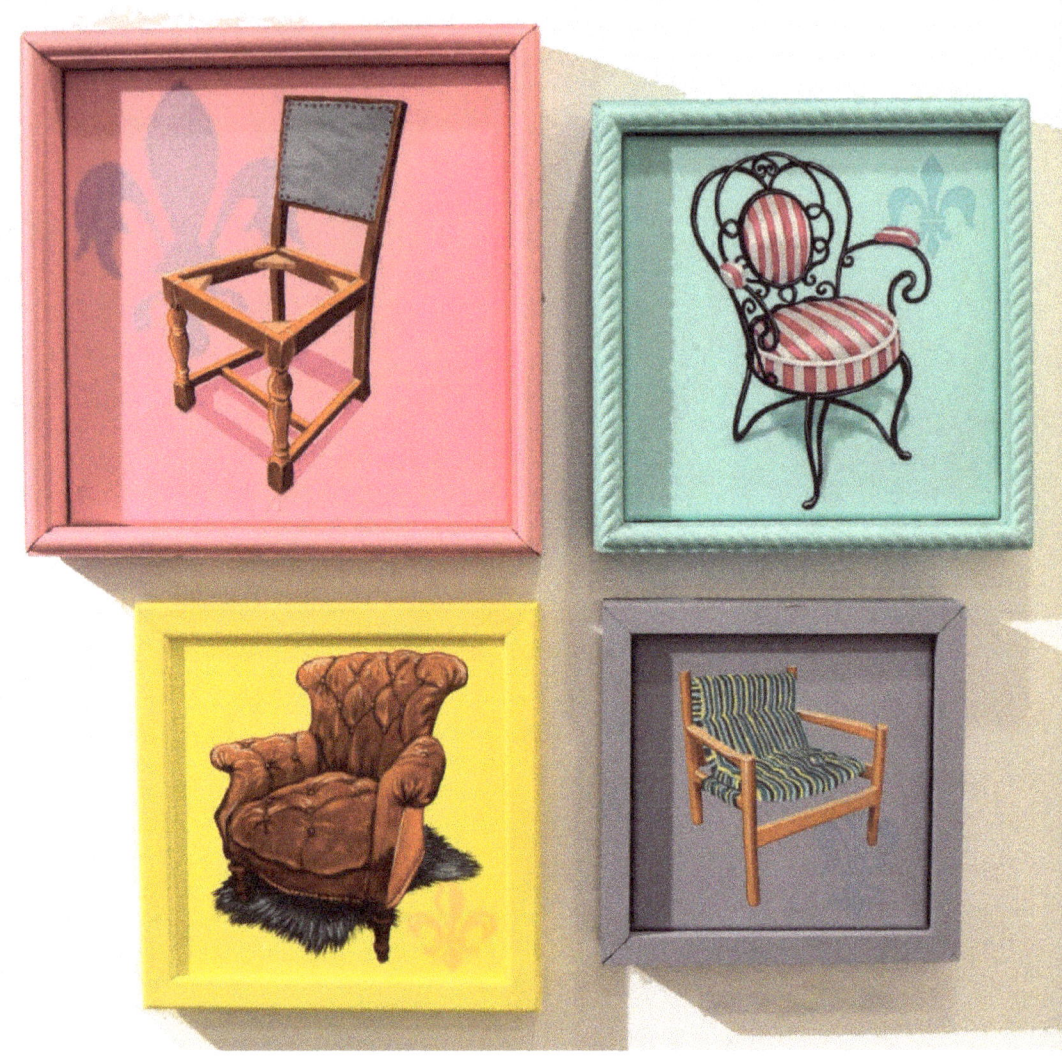

4 LOVELY CHAIRS

I paint chairs when people I love pass away.

These four symbolise four separate people who I care for that have died in the past few years. I'm not good with death. It brings out the crazy in me. It's always a real struggle for me when people say they lost someone, such as 'I lost my dad', because I just always want to say something along the lines of, 'Well that was careless! Was it in a particularly large shop? Did you bother to look?'

But I don't. I bite my lip. I hold my tongue. Fucking tempting though. Mostly because death is a sacred thing, also because I'm not totally removed from reality.

In this painting there are four very different chairs because the four people who I am referring to had four very different personalities.

Death is a shit. I think about it a lot, I think we all do, we just don't bring it up in conversation (but we should).

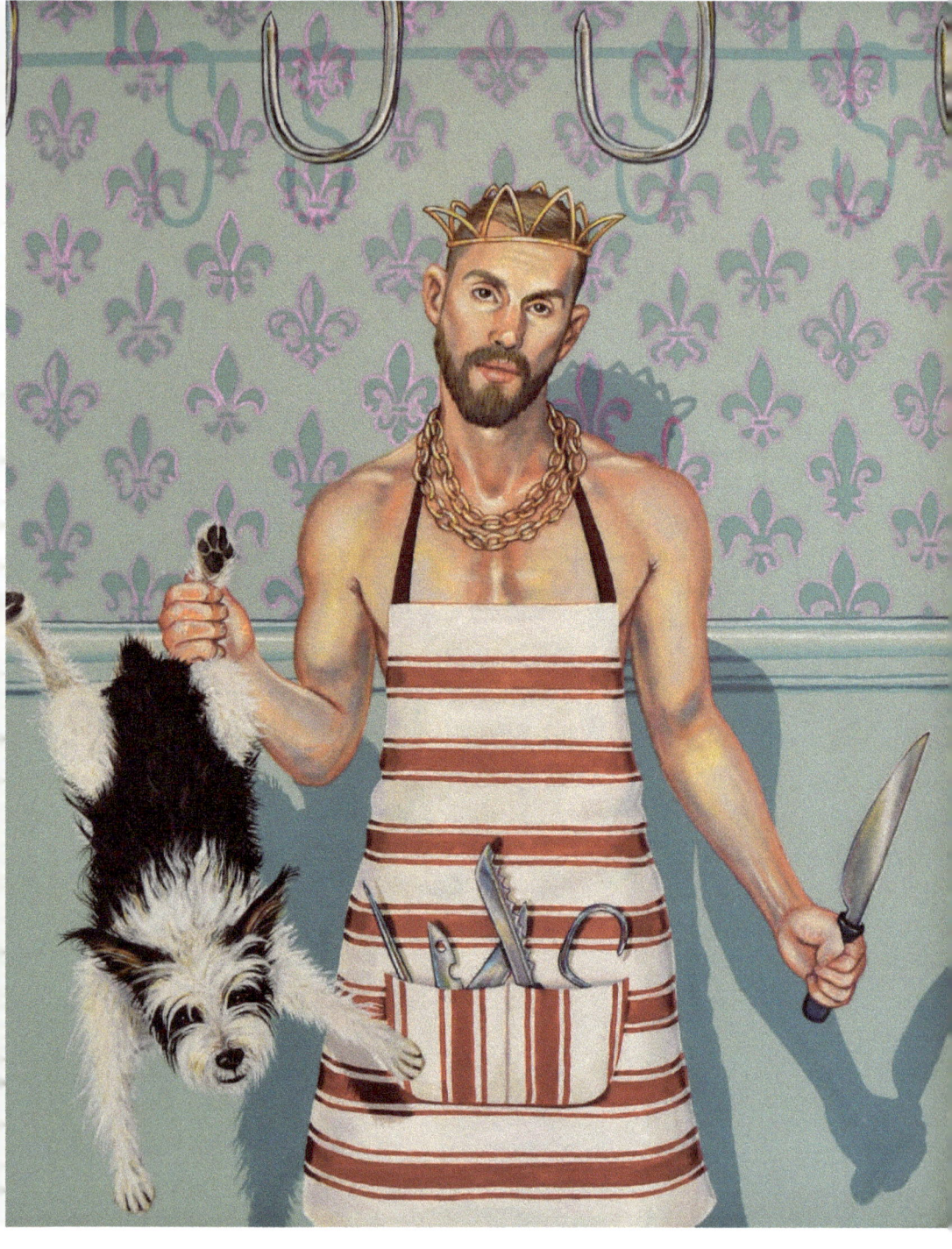

HAVING A
FRIEND FOR
DINNER

There are two creatures I hold very dear to my heart in this painting.

The first one being my friend Luke. He is a friend of, I think about, fifteen years. When I first met him, he was in his early twenties and, I say this with affection, as dodgy as all fuck! He was the worst type of a London-geezer you ever could meet (even though I first met him here in Sydney). Ooh he'd fleece ya as soon as look at ya, he would, but with a heart of gold and the wallet of somebody else. I say this with a lot of affection. He was definitely a product of the London Estates he grew up in. Definitely an unpolished diamond. He and I connected straight away. Takes one to know one. Fast forward to now and he is a really awesome, sound as a pound, ethically driven, independent film maker; and I utterly and wholeheartedly love him to bits. He is a very tough man in some respects, but an absolute darling of one. His work is as clever and as thoughtful as he is, and it has a very sharp edginess to it that I don't think many others could bring. I would now, very mostly, trust him to hold my wallet if ever circumstances required it.

I explained to Luke what the painting was going to be before I started it. I explained to him as well, that as roguishly handsome as he was, the outcome wasn't going to be a flattering portrait of him, in as much as I was going to Disney-villain-ify him up a bit. The outcome does look like Luke, but just a colder, harder, meaner looking version.

The second favourite creature in this painting is my little furry bestest friend lil' Matey-dog. Matey is a rescue hound that my partner Ryan and I adopted a while ago and he makes our life complete. We have no idea what his upbringing consisted of, which is a shame because I bet he was the cutest little puppy dog, although there's definitely some trauma there, so it probably wasn't an idyllic puppyhood.

When I take him for a walk in the mornings (he wakes Ryan and I up every morning at some ungodly hour by walking across our bed like some short legged, bouncy, demonic mountain goat, licking our noses and sneezing into our faces) he likes to do his morning poo outside the very same shop each day, beside where we live. I have no idea why it has to be there, but that's where he likes to drop anchor, so to speak. When we first got him, I noticed he'd always get really anxious whilst pooing as if fearing some surprise attack. So I'd sing to him so he knew I was there and keeping a lookout for him. The song I'd sing is, 'Matey you're a stinker, Matey you're a stinker, Matey you're a stinker and you've got a stinky clinger!' He likes it and now, so do I. It's my happy song. He poos a lot free-er knowing I'm there, keeping guard. I shall also point out various passersby have also laughingly commented on the beauty of my morning song.

(Other songs in my repertoire include such worldwide smashes as 'You is a doggie, yes you is' and 'You like the little treatsies and you got cute little feetsies, you is Maaaaaaatey dog!' Go buy the 'Best of and Greatest Hits of Matey songs', out now on Doggiepoosongs records!)

He is the cutest, friendliest, most anxious little thing, and is worshiped as the fluffy god he is, by myself and many of my friends.

I wanted him to look slightly cartoon-like in this painting, I was aware before I painted it that it's quite a disturbing image, and I thought his comedy cuteness might de-unpleasantness it. I purposefully dialed down the use of bright colours, although I intentionally made the stripes on the apron blood red. Initially I had imagined a slightly different picture: I wanted Luke, in a blood splashed apron, holding a piglet in one hand and Matey in the other and was going to call the painting 'Why eat one and sing to the other?', but that title, although, making sense in this explanation, was a bit cryptic and since I also don't have any piglets to paint at hand, I compromised a smidge. You cut your cloth to suit your weave, and Luke ended up holding a butcher's knife, which I think creates a softer more ambiguous scene.

You know that joke, how do you know if someone is vegan? Oh, don't worry, they'll tell you. Well, I've been vegan for a few years now, although I actually forget that it's a thing and that I'm in a minority (ooh another one?). Matey isn't vegan yet, but we are doing our bestest to vegan-ise him bit by bit. He still has an addiction to the old chicken biscuits, which is understandable. Although we have no real idea what happened in his life before he was 'rescued' from the pound, I'm quite sure his diet has always been a standard dog-food one.

However, I think with time, love and the power of moving songs about clinkers, we can bring him to the light. So far, his favorite food-stuffs are potatoes (any way they come, but FYI oven roasted is preferred) peas, black beans, pasta bake (oh my gawd he fucking loves his pasta bake) chickpeas, apple crumble and anything we leave within his reach whilst we look away (which is exactly how we found out he loves apple crumble).

He is a mix of breeds (we have a rough idea of what, and we are still convinced there is a bit of mountain goat and racoon in there somehow). And he has a little stumpy tail that never stops wagging, he is such a happy little dog.

A common theory, and one I wholeheartedly share is that all oppression is linked. If you are racist, then there's a very good chance you are sexist, ableist, ageist, and also speciesist in various degrees too. Speciesism is when you value the life or wellbeing of one species (humans) over the rest of the animal kingdom. I'm constantly surprised and disappointed how many people call themselves animal lovers while happy to chow down on a burger without giving it any thought. I once utterly lost my shit at a woman demonstrating against abortion outside a women's clinic who, and I kid you fucking not, was holding a big sign saying 'All life is sacred' WHILST EATING A BURGER!

For this year's No Meat May campaign that Ryan and I run, we were going to get a tiny No Meat May T-shirt printed up for Matey and have photos of him as our 'ambassadog' with the slogan 'No Meat Matey—if he can do it so can you!' And we still might do that in coming years, but since we'd only had him a few months, we decided he wasn't quite ready yet to be thrust into the international spotlight. We just wanted him to settle in before we made him work for his keep. This painting, as far as I know is his modelling debut. But because he's a rescue dog, who really knows …

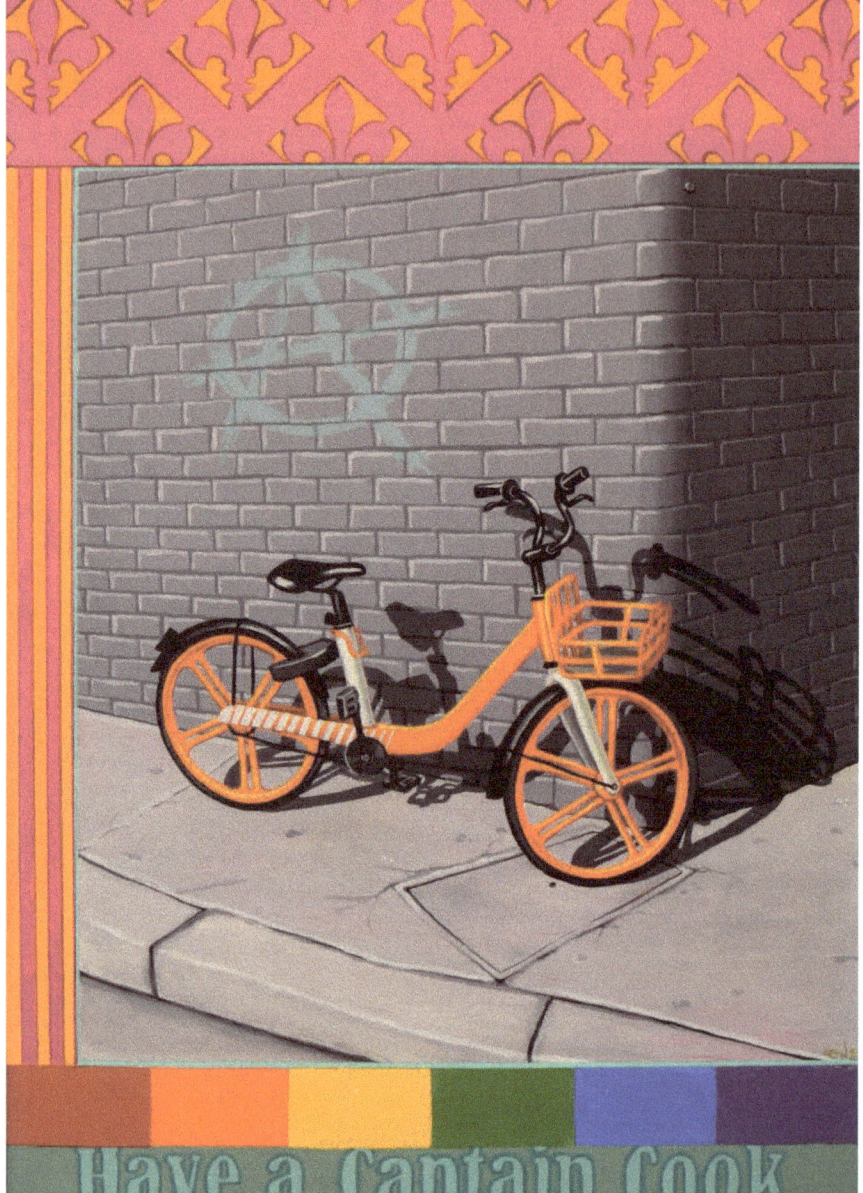

Have a Captain Cook

HAVE A
CAPTAIN
COOK

I love particular words. I also love how they sound in different accents. I imagine the title of this painting being said in a real Cockney geezer kind of accent. 'Having a Captain Cook' being Cockney rhyming slang for 'Having a look around'. Certain words just sing on their own. The word Glabella is the name for the space between your eyebrows. It's such a glorious word isn't it? Glabella. Roll it round your tongue. Such a joyous and sensuous word, so abundant in richness. And Ragamuffin, Elderberry, Pumpernickel, Kerfuffle, are all such wonderful words too. Say them out loud and say them slow read them aloud like a sexy telephone operator. I want to bathe in them, I want to roll around in them and let them fingerbang me while holding eye contact. Fingerbang is such a cheeky and saucy word, definitely open to interpretation and could be a crowd divider to say the least, but I like it.

Bidialectal is also one of my tip-top all-time favourite words. Bidialectal. If somebody is bidialectal it means they may use two dialects, or accents, as they speak with different people, perhaps from different regions, backgrounds or class brackets. I was born up in Northumberland in the North East of England and moved down to London when I was eighteen. Since the very first day of being driven down to London by my Dad, I would definitely say I've been bidialectal. Up until that point I'm sure I would have had a standard regional 'Geordie' accent. However, having, what I believed, at the time, to be a common sounding regional accent in London, just didn't tie into who I wanted to be, and ooh, I certainly did not want to be the person I grew up being. Abused, bullied, persecuted, these aren't either pleasant words or enjoyable experiences. I don't ever want to roll around and be violated or shaped by those particular words ever again. Been there, done that. In my twenties, whenever I went back to the North East, less pronounced than it once was, my accent would return, I would feel it oppressively return like some unconscious, yet futile, attempt at assimilation. However sure enough whenever I was returning to London, back on the train south, round about Leeds or Yorkshire my Geordie accent would instinctively lift away from me like a traumatised soul leaving its body.

Like I say, bidialectal; one of my favourite words.

I don't know if my voice really changed that much, since I moved to Sydney, back at the end of the last century. Whenever I phone or video call my friends and family back in the UK they love to tell me I have an Aussie accent; they are probably right, but I can't hear it. I would be happy if it was true, I suppose. I'm rather quite content with who I am right now.

Often when I do interviews people tell me I speak too slowly, but I always prefer to think about what I have to say. Our choice of words can be a very loaded weapon and we should unsheathe that weapon carefully.

Unsheathe, that's also a beautiful word.

The writer in me loves words and the painter in me loves colours! Notice how I didn't say particular colours, I'm a bit of a colour-loving-slut, I love all colours! Chromatophilic would be my correct title for this love, although I don't exactly love how that word sounds, too many pointy edges—too erratic and triangular.

I'd happily let most colours fingerbang me. Orange is possibly my favourite colour, but then who can't appreciate the depth of a dreamy, slightly muted purple, a gloriously vibrant bright red or a joyous bright primary yellow. Some colours even have sumptuous names: Indigo, makes me think of dreamy washes of dark velvety blue winter skies. Ultramarine, not a colour I use much of unless to mix, but the name rolls nicely and encourages deep sumptuous depths. Vermillion: love the colour also love the way the word sounds so like both a threat and a curse. I don't really ever use a lot of plain black in my paintings I find a dark purple or delicious coco brown gives a warmth that true black just doesn't contain, but that's not to say I don't appreciate its power.

I love being male bodied, too. To me, being male is determined, sexy, ambitious and, occasionally, dominant. However, I never follow gender stereotypes and I don't let my gender, intentionally lead me in most situations. I always try to let compassion and creativity lead me in most situations. I love dwelling in the feminine side of myself. To me being a queer man allows me to embrace the feminine energy that is available to me. I identify as Gender Non-conforming and that mindset encourages me to tap into my empathetic and imaginative side, which traditional (read fucked up and dull) masculinity doesn't really encourage. When I am at my strongest, I am usually tapping into my feminine side as I was surrounded by strong women growing up, and theirs is the kind of strength I admire and aspire too.

Faggot! Now there's a word that makes a statement. I've actually learned to love that word, but more about that bad-boy later.

So, you see, I have a foot in a few camps. I see the world from a few angles, and I encourage myself to walk as openly as I can in the world with these elements of myself exposed and I try to appreciate as much as I can as I go.

I hope that doesn't Bamboozle you or Flummox you too much. They are marvellous words aren't they! Concoction! Appreciation! Whatchamacallit! Scatter! Lethargic! I hope me being me doesn't cause you too much of a Hullabaloo or Flabbergast you too much, otherwise this opulent book about my extravagant, yet lethargic ragamuffin shenanigans probably isn't for you.

People often ask why I keep painting bikes again and again, but you see I love the form of them, sometimes I love the colour of them, and I always love the potential of them: static, unlocked, open and available to take you away on any adventure. Potential is such a good word, isn't it? It doesn't sound too spectacular, but to me it's such a potent and encouraging word.

Potential. It's a mixing colour, but one that can add to any tone or scene.

I've experienced so much in my life and I process a lot of that through my paintings. As a child I never had my potential explained to me, I always felt really quite worthless growing up. Very rarely did I feel like I could grow up to be someone that had worth, but here I am. I always understood my potential and I think painting bikes is my way, via colour or a secret code, of reminding others to always see and stay open to their potential also. Appreciate colour, love form, roll around in words, and claim who you are and can be. It's never too late. Sometimes those around us might not understand it, so I advise adapting to bidialectalism and searching out people who appreciate what you have to say, regardless of how you say it.

I once lost a sale at an exhibition on an opening night because a 'potential buyer' (those two are some of my very favourite words when used together) asked about why I often paint bright orange bikes against a warm grey background and I cheerily informed them that, to me, those colour combinations are about liberation and freedom. The grey is a particular grey used in uniforms by the German Army in the 2nd World War. The uniform grey scale in question is called *Feidgrau*.

Feidgrau, a beautiful word and colour, but the ugliest of ugly stories behind it.

Now obviously, I completely understand that particular colour reference is a loaded and powerful thing, but to me, art, or at least the art I make, is about taking colours, words, memories and actions that could be used to oppress and degrade us and taking those things and making something new and beautiful that makes us appreciate who we are, unlocking our potential, what we can do and what we can say. Potential; such a powerful word.

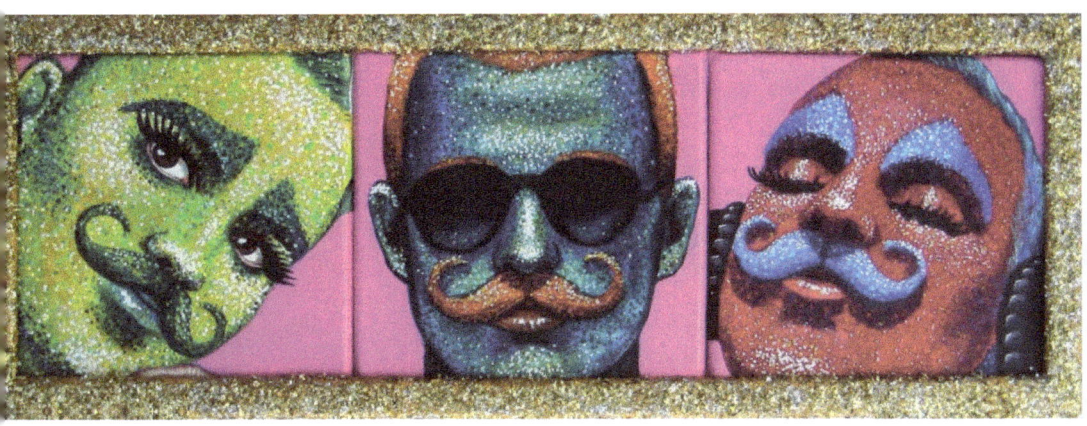

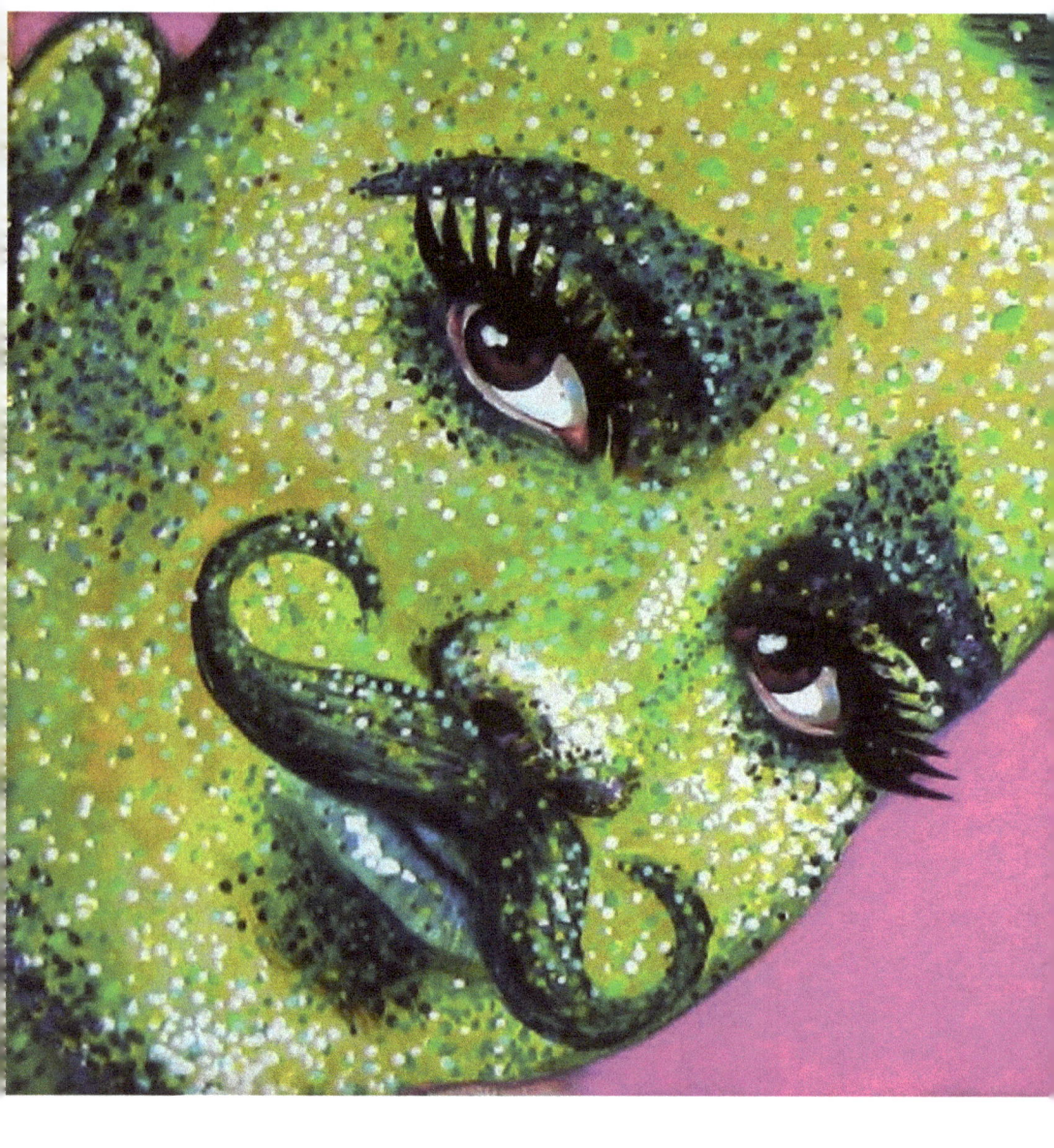

TRIPTYCH OF THE GAY GLITTER GANGSTER

This is a triptych of my good friend Kieran. They identify as Non-binary, so their pronouns are *they* and *them*. They are a performance artist and they often perform in galleries, dressed quite outrageously, with a full face of glitter make-up and, without music playing, they walk up and start dancing and gyrating with regular gallery attendees.

Is it art? Not sure. Is it fun? Fuck yeah!

It is rather amusing to watch them do their thing, although once in a packed gallery they came and danced next to me and started pulling on me to start dancing with them and I almost died of embarrassment. I still think it was fun for everybody else, though, seeing me panicking and trying to slap them away! The hussy!

I've been meaning to do a portrait of Kieran for a long time, but have always dreaded asking them around to my studio because I actually rather fucking hate glitter, urgh, I tell you, it really is the herpes of the craft world! Glitter just won't leave once you invite it in, it gets into every nook and cranny (or every crook and nanny, depending on your lifestyle choices); also I know it takes Kieran ages and lots of effort to put on a full face of glitter and I felt guilty asking them to do so just so they could sit in my studio with an audience of one.

Because of Lockdown I managed to sidestep the glitter in every crevice concern, and I asked Kieran to send me a few of their favourite photos and I worked from them. Much easier and with a lot less brushing-up and swearing afterwards. I did try to keep them involved though with constant updates and allowing them to choose the name of the painting. Their title choices were:

Gay Glitter Gangster
Glitter, Glitter and Glittererier
My front door looks like a back door

Now, clearly there's a need to explain that third option there. A few days after Halloween Kieran and I were talking about Trick or Treating children, and, without thinking, Kieran said the words 'I don't always get much action because my front door looks like a back door'. And that made me utterly lose my shit, as I believe most people would. I chuckled like a drain for almost an hour. Kieran was a tad less amused than I was, but still saw the funny side of it. I love Kieran to bits, they don't seem to mind, like me, when they are the butt of the joke. A few different times Kieran has called me an 'elder' or their 'queer fairy godmother', which I really appreciate and allows me a lot of rope when it comes to ribbing them! I like having queer and queerly minded friends who all get each other and without explanation will get gay humour and not take offense at the careless throwing of catty humour or shade.

Masculinity is a constantly recurring theme in my work, or rather a lot of my work is about portraying alternative ideals to traditional masculinity. A lot of times in my life I have struggled getting through situations or experiences and I find the traditional idea of masculine behaviour just doesn't produce good results in my world (or in my art). Certainly, when I employ traditional masculine ideals it can lead to more trouble than not. For example, I don't mind being the butt of the joke or the person everyone is laughing with or at, I find myself hysterically funny, so why wouldn't everyone else? Yet this isn't a very masculine thing to do; to accept being directly laughed at.

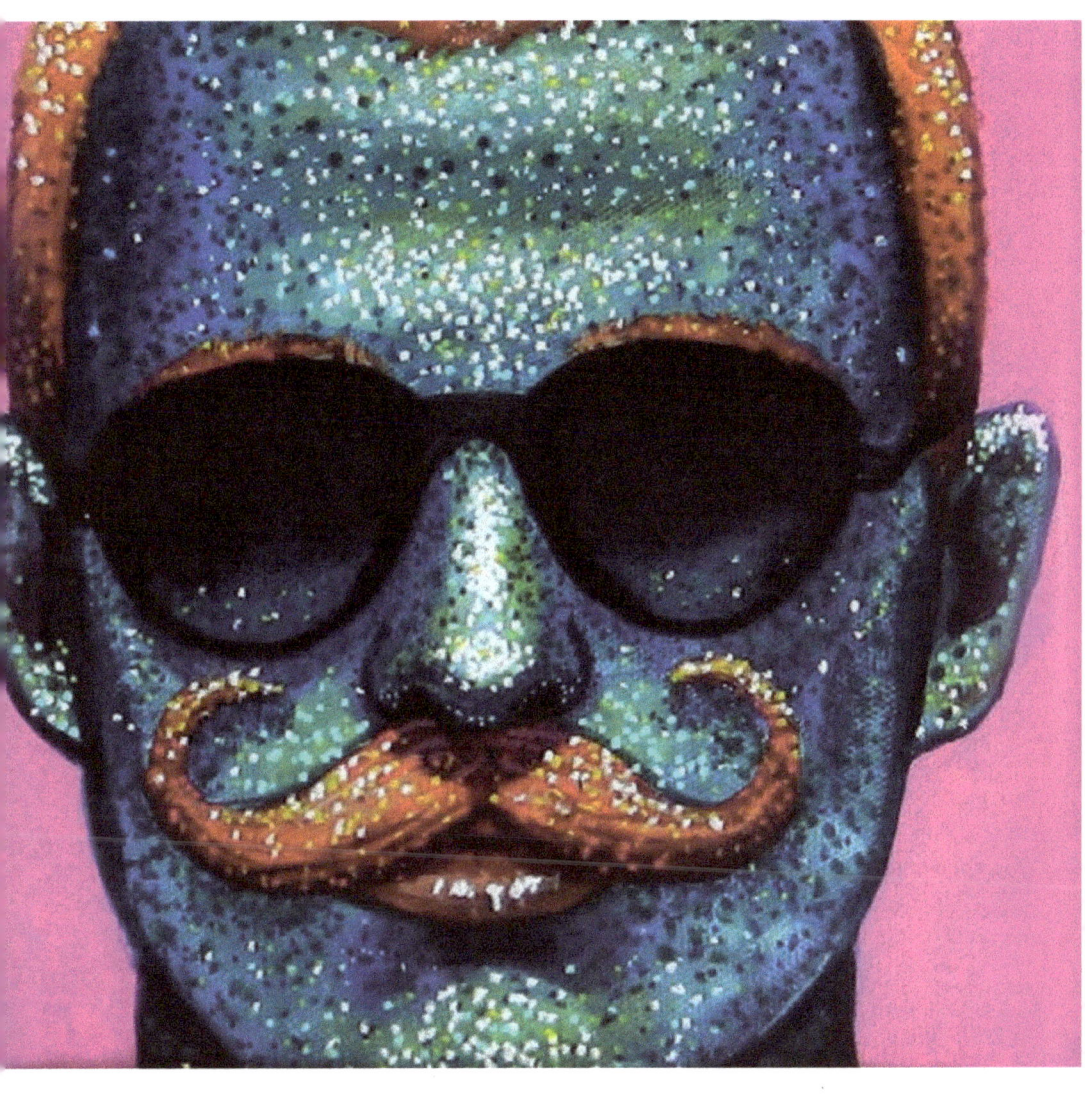

When I approach situations with compassion, openness and gentleness, then I find I can normally get through, solutions appear and sometimes I can even thrive within or because of what the world throws at me. This is my second book, however I had already written what I thought would be my second book before I even started my first. A few years ago, I started a project called *What Maketh A Man* and it has never really felt finished. It just kept evolving and the subject matter itself kept educating me as to different ways to approach the project. Initially it was a series of sketches depicting new ideals of what physical masculinity could look like. I found that straight men hardly ever, if at all ever, see other men naked (certainly not outside the locker room where neanderthal bravado and dumb-fuckery rule). The sketches I undertook were a series of non-sexual but honest depictions of male identifying individuals that were happy to be interviewed about how traditional masculinity had shaped their movement in the world, and whether or not it had actually helped them. The sketches then progressed into an exhibition, a series of audio recordings, a documentary, and a book, however none of these projects are completely finished as I really struggle to get a definitive ending; I mean realistically, could I really ever? Masculinity and its effects in the modern (certainly Colonial) world are massive, if not endless. Could I ever truly have absolute closure or definitive views on a project so vast and incredibly omnipresent with such massive outcomes?

My challenge of masculinity really stems from having been not made to feel good enough (or butch enough) as a child. I was a constant disappointment to others, especially dear old Dad. Even back then I knew I shouldn't care about letting people down, but as a child that is a difficult thing to structure and express. Certainly in my working class family in the area and time I grew up, I was seen as a letdown because of my lack of obvious masculinity. As is often the case it became a bit of a downward spiral.

I was always told by my dad to change how I spoke; 'Talk like a man,' he would often shout at me, but the reality was I just didn't understand what that meant. Was it the tone, was it the accent or was it the words I chose, was it the over flamboyant use of the words darling and fabulous? Possibly, although in truth I just had no idea where I was actually going wrong. Possibly it was because the men I were drawn to as role models weren't men who would talk at all like my father, so I was left torn as to what 'real men' talked like.

Decades later I still have a lack of confidence about my voice, it's complex, but now thrown into the mix is not just how I sound or what I'm saying, but it's whether or not my voice even has any need to be heard; surely at best I'm just another ego driven cis white man with a set of self-gratifying opinions? Why is a part of the typically male arsenal not knowing when to let others speak before you? I know I can be overbearing and over forceful with opinions and views; we all can, but learning early to edit myself and know when to keep *shtum* has actually turned out to be a good thing! Being unsure about my own voice has encouraged good listening skills.

When I was growing up I had three clever elder sisters and four fabulously strong and interesting aunties, I was proud to talk with them, like them, and consider their views. My aunties worked in factories, had big hair and took no nonsense from men. God they really were fabulous! Women from the North of England can be naturally formidable and quick witted as all hell! I remember feeling so proud of my eldest sister when, as a teenager, I once saw her quickly grab a lipstick from her bag and apply it perfectly without a mirror, (instant life goals!) I mean, wow, that's independence and resourcefulness right there!

However, that's not to say I was deprived of male or masculine role models. I had cousins, uncles, teachers and classmates a plenty, I just never saw one that I wanted to emulate. Some of them I didn't mind, and I hope their lives and coping skills worked for them; but I never saw myself reflected in who they were or were becoming or

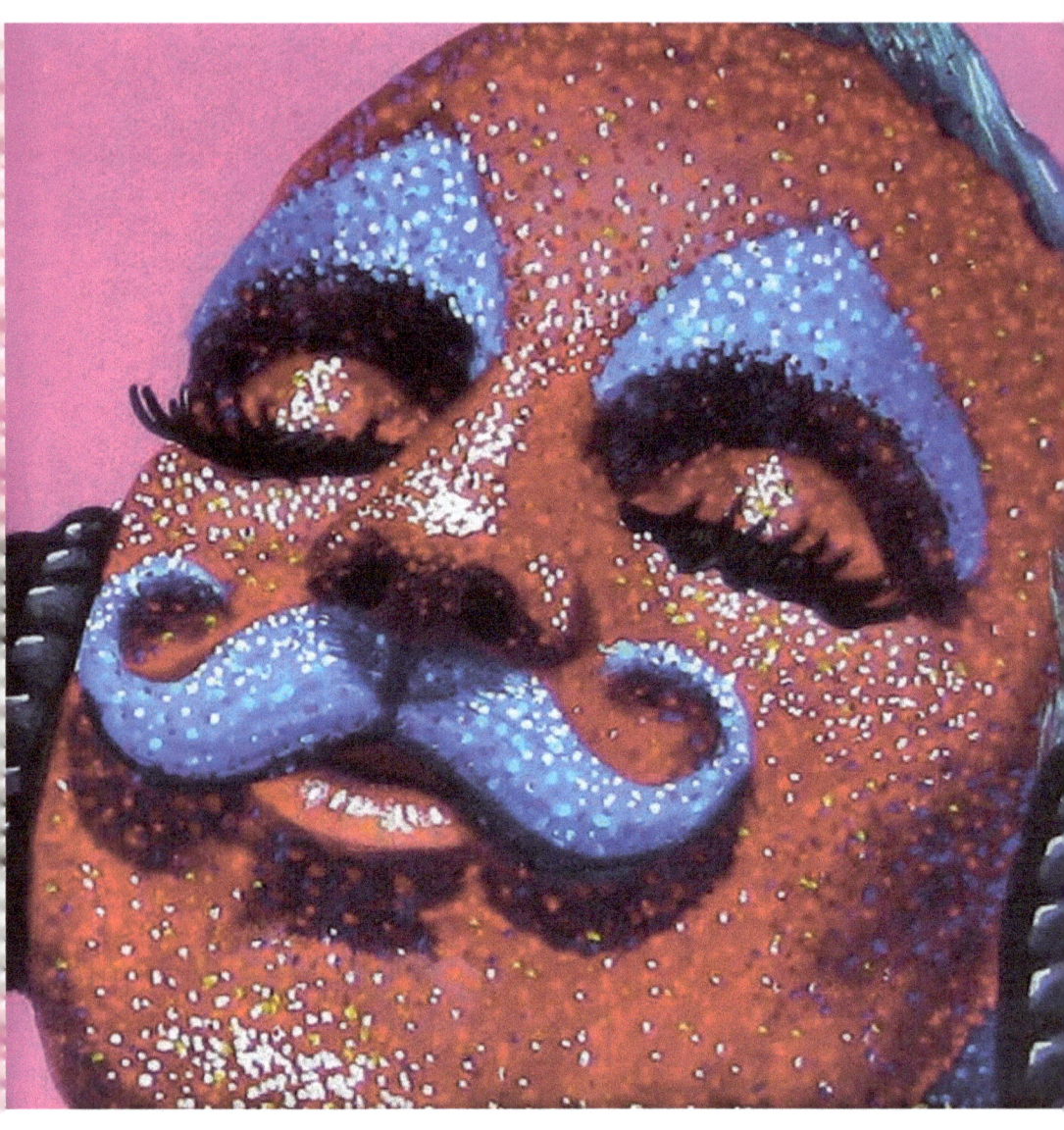

aiming to be. Their goals in life were never mine. I'm painting with a broad brush here, obviously, but you understand my point. My biggest struggle as a child was not conforming into the role that most others saw I should fill, I just wasn't naturally drawn towards typically male pastimes like sport, cars or punching things.

To me the difference was that women would often be independent and resourceful when called upon, but men rarely, if left to their own devices. The men I knew were always driven by ego at best and held back by failure at worst; they always needed encouragement and wanted validation. Women just got on with stuff and made situations work. The men I knew always wanted a slap on the back and a team of mates to loudly celebrate victories with and, although these things were never truly available to me, they were also achievements I never aspired to. Women talked about feelings and processed emotions, men talked about football and how fucking awesome it was being men. As a teenager I slowly learnt how to structure not worrying about what people thought of me, but it was hard and challenging.

Even though I never aspired to be typically or predictably male I was always happy enough in my male body and I always knew, even from a young age, that I was thoroughly attracted to men. Whenever my father would enforce the watching of a football match in the hope of making me interested in manly sports, I would always wander off uninterested, yeah yeah, kick the ball, kick the ball, fabulous, well done chaps! Yet funnily enough, I'd be slap-bang in front of the TV when at half time and at the end, when there was footage of the changing room and shirtless footballers! I would literally have my nose pressed against the screen. Nowww you've got my attention. Can't think why my Dad was concerned …

But no matter how many football matches and masculine pastimes were offered up to me, I never did learn to 'talk like a man'. As I said, years later, I'm still worrying about and considering how my words resonate in the world and that's certainly an ongoing process, maybe I'll never not have that issue. I have, nevertheless, learnt to combine this with an ongoing lack of concern about what people think of me. If I'm judged by what commonly makes a man, I'll fail every time, but if I'm assessed about being creative, resourceful and compassionate, then a more accurate picture could appear.

The *What Maketh A Man* project still plods on, no real end in sight. I will try to publish the book at some point soon, maybe as my next book. The documentary, though, is very problematic—it's already on it's third director. Funnily enough, other people also struggle with the enormity of the subject matter too, but honestly, if this ends up being my life's work, so be it. I have so much to process around the questions of 'what is masculinity?' and 'what does modern masculinity (or post-masculinity) look like?'

Kieran chose the first title, The Gay Glitter Gangster, but in my head, whenever I see the painting, the third unofficial title makes me chuckle.

I once saw a drag queen respond to a group of men heckling her from a moving car by shouting, 'I'm more of a woman than you'll ever have and I'm more of a man then you'll ever be!' Fabulous! Although I actually don't want to aim for either of those ideals, I'm happy in my own space roughly existing between typically male and female ideals. I don't identify as Gender Neutral as Kieran does, but I do identify as gender non-conforming. I am fine with the pronouns of *his* and *him*, but only my own definition of that, no one else's. If I disappoint you, if I'm less than you expect or want me to be, then that's your concern, not mine, and feel free to move on, but before you do, watch this; I also can flawlessly put on lipstick without a mirror!

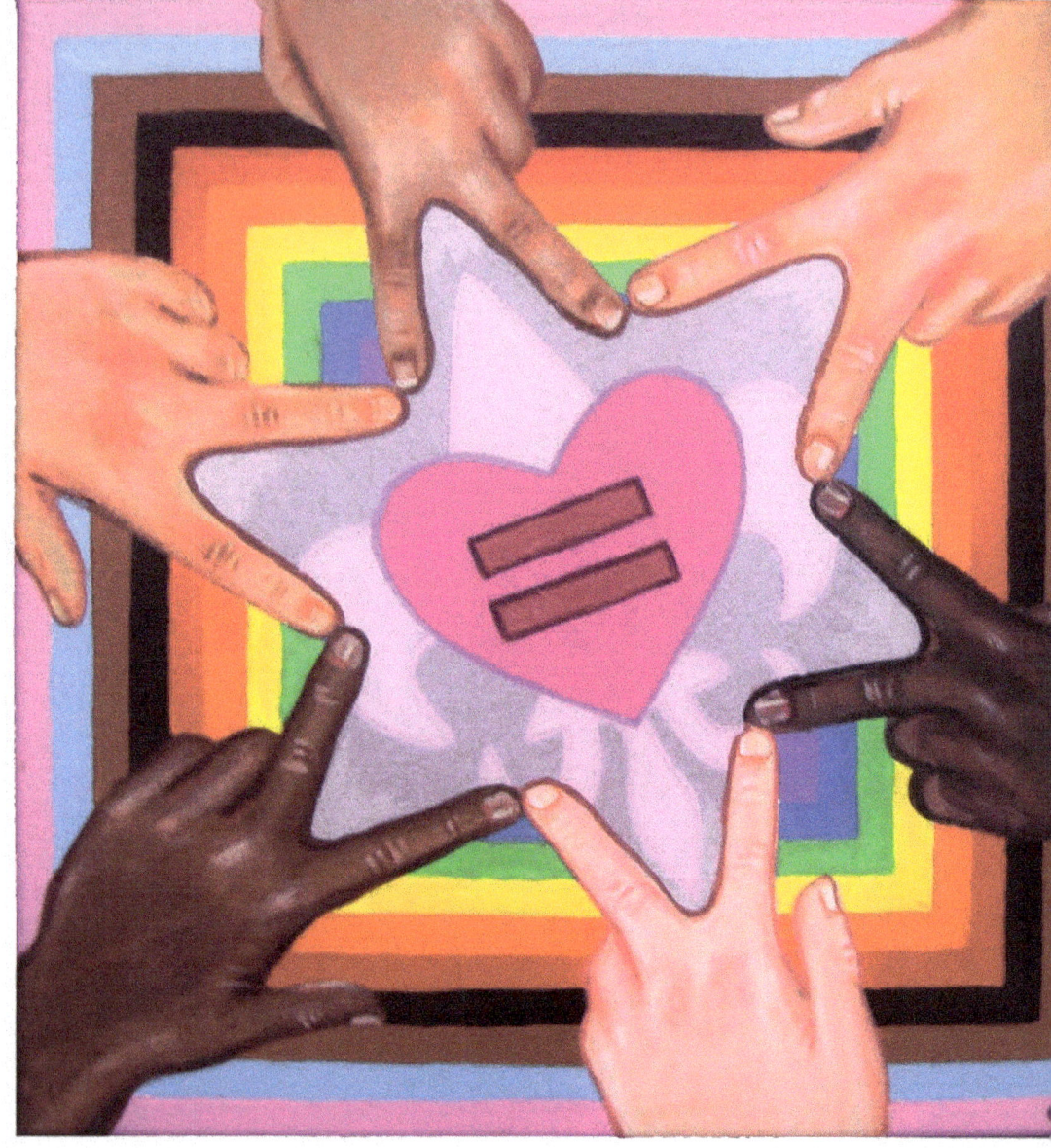

TOGETHER WE MAKE STARLIGHT

This is a piece I painted so I could sell it and copies (digital and prints) specifically to pass on all money raised to a number of First Nations charities.

I know money isn't the answer but it's a major part of helping people who can change things change things.

I often get accused of 'virtue signalling' in my work and I would like to address that below:

Go fuck yourself.

If you think I'm virtue signalling, then absolutely fine, but go do the same and try making a difference yourself, before you criticise (anyone or) me.

We can all do better, I'm no different and I am the first to admit there is room for improvement in every element of who I am and what I do.

But I actively try to make myself open to learning and open to activating better ways of being.

Thank you for coming to my TED talk.

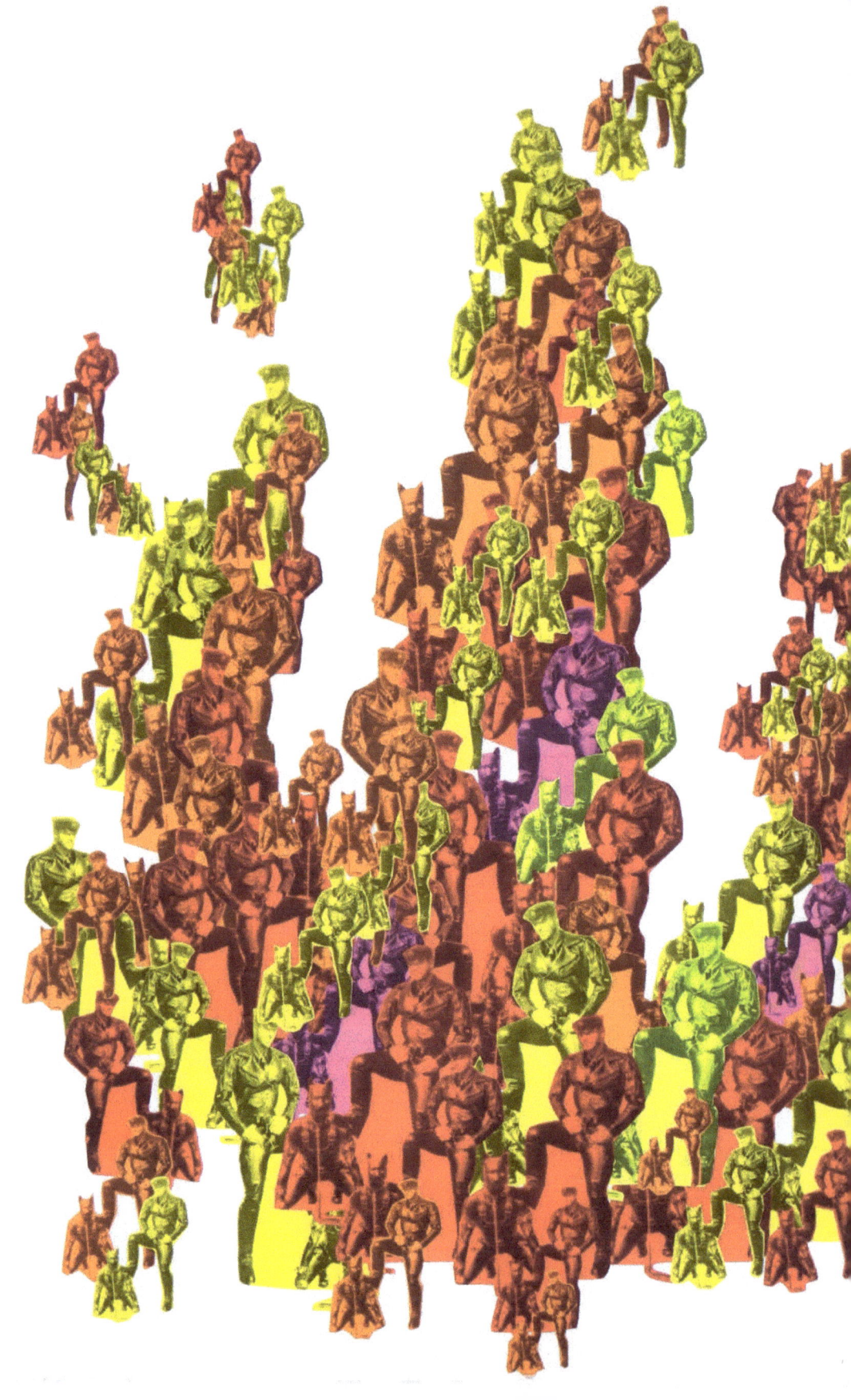

LEATHERMAN MADE CLIMATE CHANGE

So, and this might be the gayest thing I've ever written, but here goes: isn't collage fabulous!

And just to confirm that we are on the same creative page here, collage is the cutting out and sticking down of ready-printed images to compose a new image. Oh my, if you have never tried it, please do, what fun!

It's kind of strange that, as someone who spends a lot of time being a professional creative, I would choose another creative project as a hobby, but I like the idea of taking something already in existence (so much easier than starting from scratch) and improving on it!

And call me shallow if you will, but it doesn't harm that collage is rather 'hip with the cool-kids' at the minute. If you search #collage on Instagram, Pinterest or TikTok (OMG, get me, I'm so freakin down with the kids) you'll find endless cool and inspirational stuff.

I co-run a fortnightly drawing group for LGBTQI Elders here in Sydney, and I'm always on the lookout for activities that are both easy and exciting. And, lemme tell you, collage ticks those boxes a treat! Inexpensiveness, readily available materials, instant results and a visual narrative should we choose to introduce one. However, there's a bit of a hurdle to navigate before introducing the attendees of the drawing group to the joyous reveal of my new creative pastime.

Now I hate to be a Debbie-downer-party-pooper here, but unfortunately there is a badly cut out dark cloud that looms over the silver-lined picnic of collage: namely all the future landfill fixtures needed to do it! I know, I know, it's a buzz kill isn't it; environmental concern alert! There's always that one annoying fool at a house party who's in the kitchen whingeing/screaming hysterically about 'don't use the plastic cups, they'll never decompose and they strangle all the turtles', when all you want to do is just pour a gin and tonic and tell them to shut up.

But it's true, plastic cups will NEVER decompose! And this is the thing, likewise, have you ever tried to find resharpenable scissors in the modern word that can be bulk-bought without plastic handles? And don't even get me started on how those little single-use plastic-encased glue sticks aren't refillable and have to be totally replaced after the miniscule blobs of glue inside have been used up!

But you know, although it's difficult, I want to try and do this properly, and not just add to the devastation of our worlds' resources, because if, whilst introducing people to the joys of creativity, in reality, I'm just adding the destruction of our world, then I'm not really doing it right, am I?

Okay, I'm going to be honest, I've kind of lured you into this written piece under false pretences. This piece isn't just about the light-hearted frolicsome joys of collage, but about how we, the LGBTQI population of this planet, are actually perfectly placed to be the ones to save it.

Aint no doubt about it, whoever steps forward and hands out non-plastic cups at a house party, is going to get derided, rejected and excluded by those other party attendees; but this is our superpower: we, as members of the LGBTQI communities are already completely used to that shit end of the social stick! We've already developed coping mechanisms and thick skin when it comes to being 'that person'. So really, if we aren't going to stand up for what we know is unpopular, but right, who is?

As someone who is vegan and has been 'plant based' (ie veggie or vegan) for my entire adult life, I am very used to the sinking feeling and compromise of beliefs needed to stand in a leather or fetish venue as the only one dressed in home-made vinyl or mock leather corsetry or harness. Fundamentally I love the look of the clichéd, big, Tom of Finland-esque, butch, hairy, leathered up daddy type as much as the next queen (be still my beating arse!). But compassion and consent are also ridiculously important to me, both in my real world and sexual fantasies, and the reality of that is, if you're wearing leather, the animal who's skin you are wearing was never compassionately treated and their consent was certainly never given for the torture they endured so that garment could be made for you.

There is no such thing as 'compassionately farmed' meat or leather. No animal ever wants to die.

Cognitive dissonance, it's a real thing, we all suffer from it. It is when someone doesn't connect one thing with another because of denial, or through not connecting the process to the outcome; it's blocking something out if we don't want to think about it – such as purchasing a wasteful single-use plastic glue-stick that has no other destination than to sit eternally in landfill and still claiming to be an environmentalist.

I'm really trying to stop myself from behaving in certain ways because, once I pause and think about my process, I often realise I can do better. We can all do better. There is always room for improvement and it usually really isn't that difficult.

Okay, back to lovely collage. The piece that accompanies this article is called 'Leatherman-made climate change' and is about how, at our worst, we can all engage cognitive dissonance when we chose to and when it suits us. The visual reference is a flame representing both, the burning of the Brazilian rainforests to make way for land on which to graze cattle and the Greta Thunberg quote, 'Act as if your house is on fire, because it is'. It is a piece about how we as human beings can 'other-ise' other beings to the point where they are nothing to us other than a distant part in a process to further our collection of fetishistic accessories, which, by the way has a name; it is called speciesism.

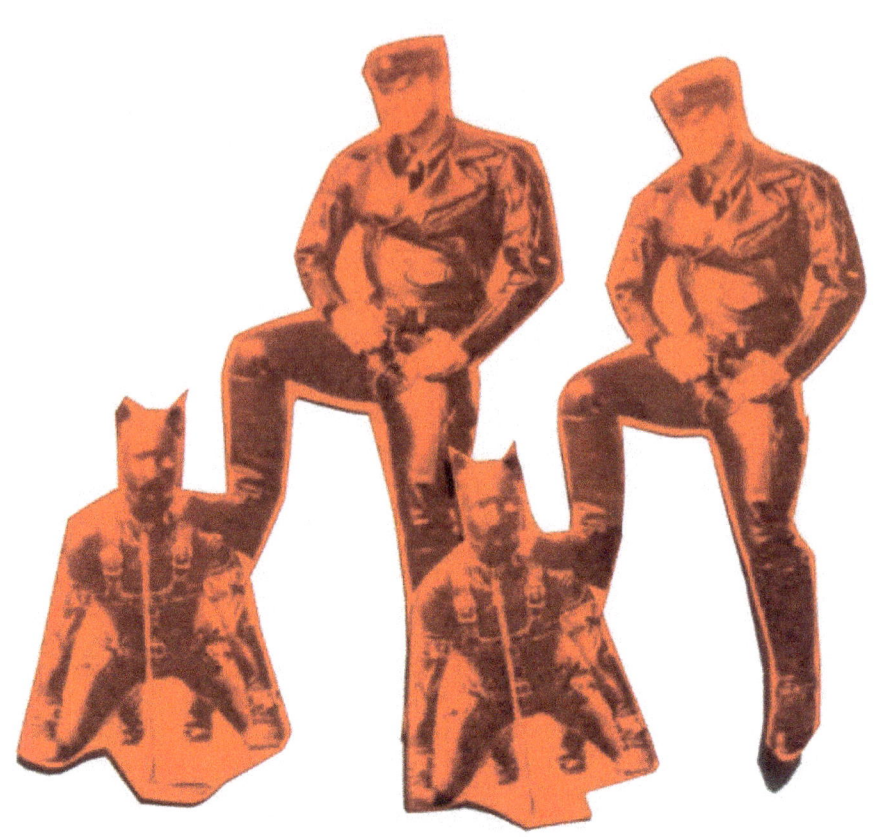

Speciesism allows us to neglectfully objectify animals and reduce them to nothing more than just meat and skin.

Cognitive dissonance is something no one wants to admit to it, but we all do it, another example of that, would be, let's say, when somebody refuses to see another person's worth because of their sexuality, I think you get the picture there. We can all do better. LGBTQI people definitely can. Let's cut speciesism out of this picture and discard it.

Years ago in my single-and-ready-to-mingle thirties I made myself a selection of good, quality vinyl harnesses (is that the correct plural for a harness, I have no idea, anyway I made several in different colours) because I wanted to go out to fetish venues and go on the sexy-hairy-daddy-hunt and oh yes madam, those homemade vinyl harnesses (and okay, I'll admit it, matching clutch bags) worked a treat thank you for asking.

I, like you, I am a complex human being who often contradicts themselves, learns as I go and I certainly am not perfect. I bought lots of glue-sticks before I thought that silliness through; now I try to use liquid PVA where I can, or I use double sided tape when it all gets a bit too tricky, but it's all still very much a work in progress, and again, I learn as I go and admit (at least to myself) when I'm wrong.

I'm aware there's a few heavy-handed metaphors in this piece, but it all forms a complete picture in the end, kind of. Like I said at the start; I like the idea of taking something already in existence (so much easier than starting from scratch) and improving on it. Collage won't save the world, only we can do that. LGBTQI people and conscious decision making built upon compassion and creative thinking rather than cognitive dissonance and needing to be popular at parties can do that.

Also, honestly, what kind of person drinks gin and tonic out of a plastic cup?

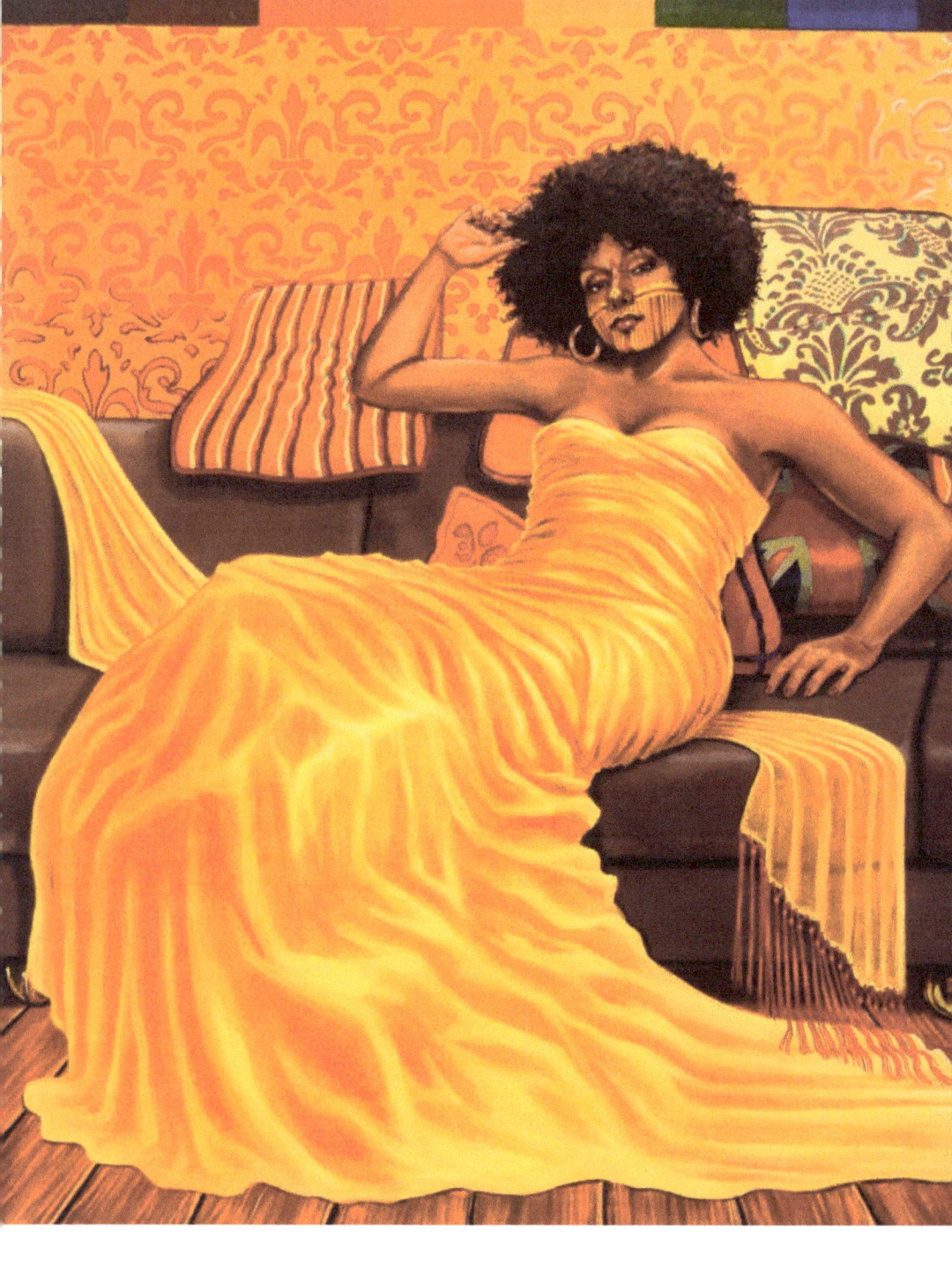

GOLD DUST WOMAN

I am my own worst critic. I beat myself up constantly over my work.

Some days, I'm just like, 'I can't write, I can't paint, I can't sing.'

Actually, I really can't sing. A few years ago I went for singing lessons at the local community college and on the very first evening all twelve students in the class had to stand in a line and collectively sing a song. The singing teacher walked the length of the line and listened to us each individually and when she got to me she stood for a while, nodded, leant in and said 'wait around at the end, I want to talk with you …'

Well, now I don't mind telling you, I have waited for this moment my entire fucking life. Obviously, she had star spotted me and I was going to be the next all-singing all-dancing pop-sensation, probably the next (forty-year-old) Justin Bieber or a chunkier, hairier Celine Dion. I'd predicted this all along, but finally the world had caught up. My time had fucking come!

In case you don't know, the title of this piece is taken from a Fleetwood Mac song and I don't mind telling you, I've always pictured myself as an easy stand in for a wabbling-voiced and scarf waving Stevie Nicks. I mean really, I'm a classic pop diva waiting to happen I honestly am!

Well, clearly my singing teacher didn't share the vision; she didn't even wait until all the other students had left when she asked if I'd ever had my ears checked!

How very dare she! Rude!

I've never been so offended in my life (although obviously I have many times)! Look, I mean yes, I kind of knew all along I wasn't the world's greatest singer, but I would have been very happy if my teacher just hadn't implied that without suggesting I was probably the worst.

I tend to be all too keenly aware of my limits. I know what I can do and what I cannot do and if I'm undecided on the issue I'll usually decide that I'm a no hoper and quit before I start. It's not an uncommon mindset.

This is a painting of my friend Mel, who is an awesome poet and performer and who has the most incredible energy. She was mentored by my friend Candy, who past-away a few years ago, and Mel shares Candy's authentic passion and power. She is so strong, fabulous and takes no nonsense from anybody. This painting is loosely inspired by Flaming June by Sir Frederic Leighton. Kind of, but not really. I love the opulence and sensuality of that painting, but the passivity of the woman in that image annoys me. Why do women in such paintings have to be so vulnerable, sleepy and soft? Floppy lady, why'st art thou so floppy?

I chatted with Mel about that painting and how I wanted to do a rethinking of that image with her—only the woman in Mel's and my painting would be defiant, questioning and resilient. She would hold the viewer to account. She wouldn't be sleepy, soft and floppy; my muse would be ready to stand her ground, ready to argue and would take no prisoners. Mel told me about how her Grandfather on her mothers' side was a chief in a Papua New Guinea tribe and we talked about trying to incorporate some of that energy into the painting.

During the preliminary sketches I wrapped Mel in a sheet in order to have reference for the fabric. I wanted the 'dress' in the painting to be open to interpretation, was it an expensive evening gown or was it a simple satin sheet. Who was this person, why was she there, what was she doing?

I pretty much finished the entire painting, but I didn't like it. There seemed to be a few unresolved areas and issues.

Mel and I had had a big conversation about anti-colonialism and we discussed the use of the Union Jack cushion in the painting. We both decided on the flag being in the background, being sat upon and reduced to a simple furnishing textile or pattern. Something to be overlooked and disregarded. Whilst I was working on the painting one day, I was listening to a podcast about the Black Lives Matter Campaign and I painted in a scarf purposely with red tassels representing rivulets of blood from just below the flag-cushion.

I kept working at the painting, but it wasn't resolving itself. There was both too much going on in it, and yet also not enough. For some reason I kept thinking back to my singing lessons, you know, maybe this was something that I just couldn't do? Maybe it was that point when you hear a singer, but the song that they are trying their best to nail is just beyond their ability, and everyone can see it but them? Well that's what I was feeling. My notes, within the painting, weren't high enough or low enough or on key, my voice was straining, the melody was a tad flat. I beat myself up a few times whist standing in front of my easel, maybe the truth of it was I just wasn't good enough to nail what I wanted to achieve.

I talked with Mel and we discussed how this woman in the painting still didn't seem sufficiently what I wanted to say. It wasn't that she was floppy, but she was still not formidable enough. Then Mel talked about how she sometimes wore her grandfather's traditional markings to perform in and *insert perfectly pitched operatic note here* everything started to come together and work as I wanted it too. The painting now made a lot more sense and the elements all began to sing in harmony.

(Am I overdoing these musical metaphors here, look I probably am, but I'm enjoying writing them!)

Undeniably when I look at this painting I still see myself skirting around the limits of my own talent, the notes are strained and there's no need for the random use of certain elements, but I'm actually fine with allowing it out into the world. I think it's part of the creative process and how we all have to push ourselves. It's not always about being pitch perfect but about getting a message and story across. I'm sure other people can see the limit to my skills clearly in this painting, but I'm fine with that.

I never really saw eye to eye with my singing teacher, she started just ignoring me in class whilst also using the term of six lessons, we twelve students had paid for, to sing over us all and plug her own upcoming live gigs. I did keep going back even though I could tell she wasn't appreciating my unrecognized talent. She gave us all homework of practicing our scales and, in the very last lesson, we were all called up before the piano to show what we could do. This was our solo, our one and only time to shine. Now in my head, my pitch was slightly off, but I was as near as my exhaustive practice had left me. However, I'll admit it, clearly, in the real world, I was massively off key. She obviously thought she would embarrass me, and after I tried to nail my notes, she proclaimed loudly in front of everyone, 'Why are you unable to sing the notes that I'm playing?' and, you know, actually I do normally get really embarrassed in front of an audience, but in this instance, I had simply stopped worrying about it and, much, much, much to the other student's amusement proclaimed, 'Actually, why are you unable to play the notes that I'm singing!'

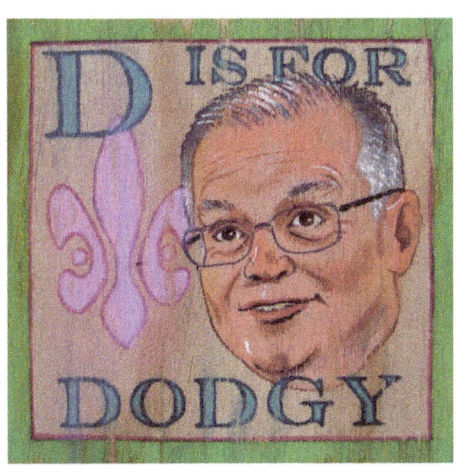

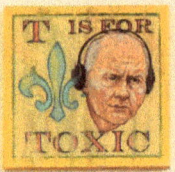

T IS FOR TOXIC

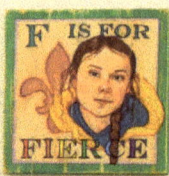

F IS FOR FIERCE

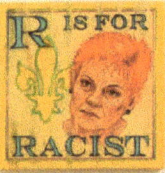

T IS FOR TALENT

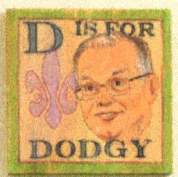

D IS FOR DODGY

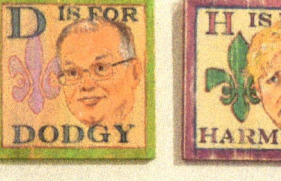

H IS FOR HARMFUL

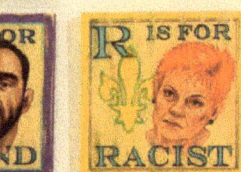

L IS FOR LEGEND

R IS FOR RACIST

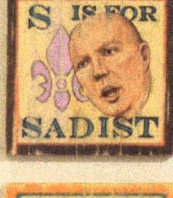

S IS FOR SADIST

P IS FOR PRIVILEGE

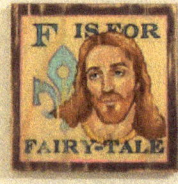

F IS FOR FAIRY-TALE

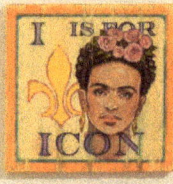

I IS FOR ICON

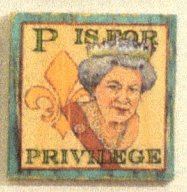

R IS FOR RESPECT

V IS FOR VILE

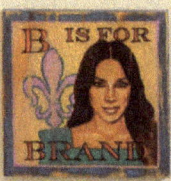

C IS FOR CULPABLE

B IS FOR BRAND

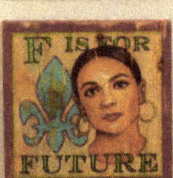

F IS FOR FUTURE

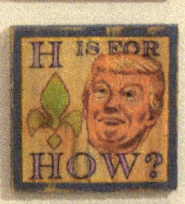

H IS FOR HOW?

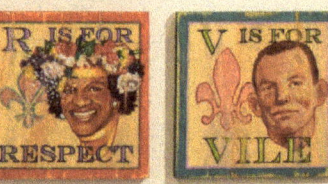

CORRUPT NOSTALGIA
SERIES

CORRUPT
NOSTALGIA

I think this series speaks for itself. It's obviously based on the idea of children's learning blocks. You know, A is for Apple, B is for big bouncy bollocks, C is for … well you get the idea, that kind of thing.

I kept the selection process quite random. People who appeared aimlessly somewhere in my thoughts appear in this series. There is no great master plan of inclusion. I didn't ever intend to do the entire 26 letters of the alphabet and I've doubled up on a few letters without thinking it all through, but you get the idea.

I wanted the negative pieces to not be reduced to a name calling exercise, but to be something that encourages the viewer to question how they view the individual portrayed.

The very first person I painted in this series was (Australian politician) Pauline Hanson, who, and I shan't hold back here, I find to be a quite repulsive person. I had a message from a friend telling me that they found the tile to be sexist as it was perpetuating the idea of negativity towards women, but at that point no one knew there was going to be a varied series and that I intended to share the negative name calling quite happily throughout all the genders. If that tile existed on its own, then yes, it would be sexist as a single punch down to a woman who obviously struggles, but as it stands, within the concept of the greater piece, I think it's okay.

But I'm also very open to hearing other people's opinion on that.

Throughout my painting of this series, I would post the new image on social media and many people had many suggestions about who else I should paint in the series and which word should be next to them. A certain male friend kept sending me suggestions of various female politicians with word suggestions, which, to put it bluntly, were absolutely downright sexist if not incredibly misogynistic. He would suggest words such as witch and hag, which made me sad because he's an intelligent fella, but just didn't fully understand how sexism and misogyny work.

As I write this, I have completed 16 tiles within this series. I might do more, I might stop there, we will see how I go. Initially they were painted for the 'Enough of your nonsense' exhibition, which (as I write this) opens in a few weeks, I may go back and continue the series after the exhibition, or I may not. That's one of the reasons I love not being tied to a commercial gallery, I just get to do whatever I want whenever I chose!

It's a funny feeling putting them out into the world. I know the Dolly tile will sell instantly, I mean, come on, who doesn't love Saint Dolly of Parton, she's an utter legend, however, I'm sure I'll be stuck with the Tony Abbott (vile is such a good word for him) one after the show. I mean realistically, who is going to want to look up and see him staring down from their wall. Although I suppose if it is hanging up in a toilet it might help keep you regular. Maybe I'll offer it free to somebody with a dungeon or sling room and hope Tony's soul becomes trapped within the portrait somehow and he is forced to look out of it forever into a big seething mass of big, glorious, hairy butch leather daddy bum-sex!!

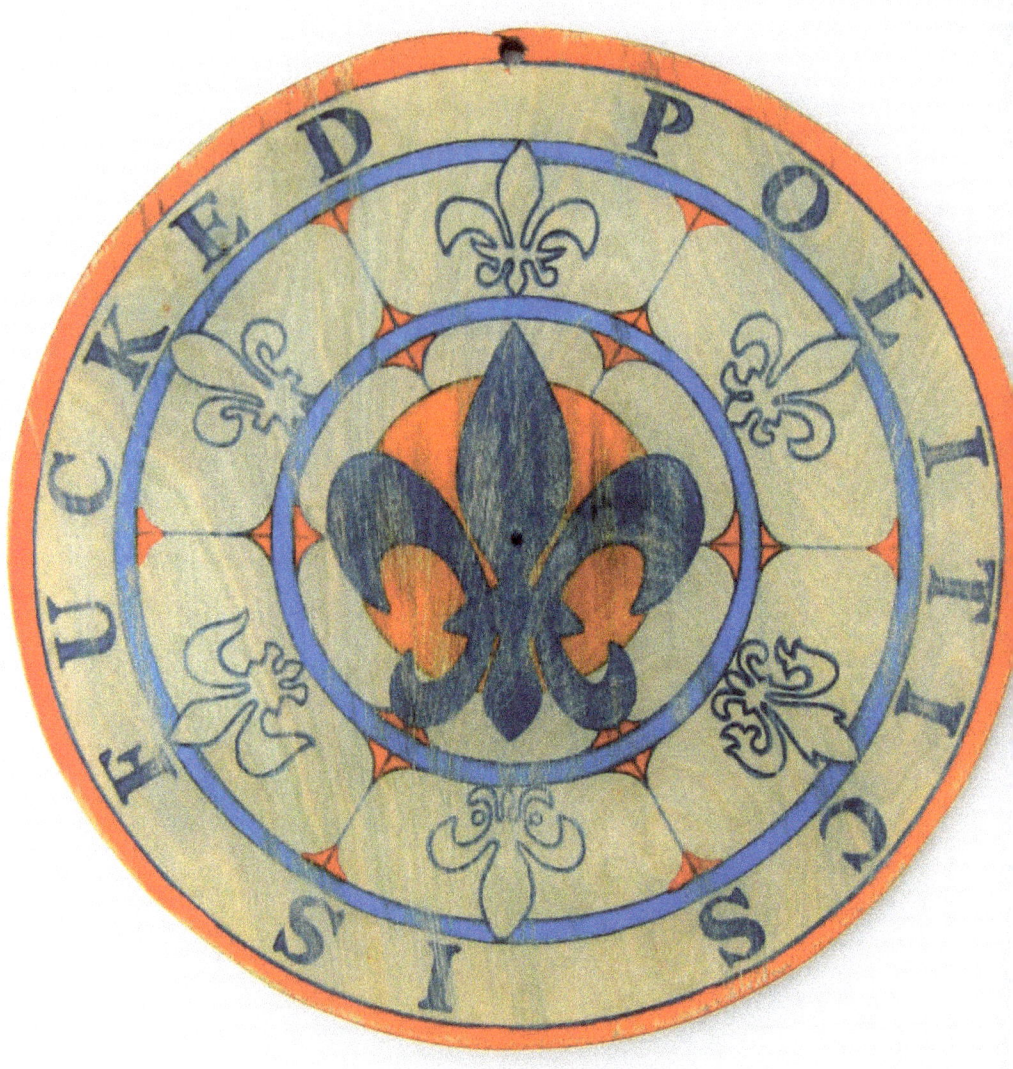

POLITICS IS FUCKED

I am aware that I am a very privileged man. I am educated, well fed, I live in a country with state run healthcare, I have a regular income, I am very able-bodied, I see representations of people like me in a positive light constantly in the media, and I get to write books and paint and indulge my silly old self, and some days I can convince myself that people are interested in what I do and decisions I make.

Although the reality is: no one really cares what I do, but you see, that's fine because what I do has no real lasting negative impact on the world, therefore it's not that important.

I mean, look, yeah, there's a fair few shit paintings that I'm responsible for, can't deny that, but no one suffers trauma or dies because of them.

However, there are some other very indulged privileged white men who make other, more important decisions, and people do die, or live in hell, because of those stupid decisions.

Hence the catchy little title behind this piece; Politics is fucked.

As a white person, the outcome of the Black Lives Matter movement affects me. I know that times they are a changing and I know, if this movement carries on as it should, my kind will definitely lose power and influence in society. My worth and influence in society will decrease. It's the same with Feminism, I'm aware of the privileges that being a man in a male centric, male-biased society brings me.

If women gain more power, perhaps as a man, I will lose some of my social standing, maybe.

However, although I'm aware I may lose out, I'm actually fine with all of the above. Fuck it, bring on the revolution! It bothers me, but not in any kind of way will I be blocking these movements, or not actively being involved in making this happen. I am all for fairness and I campaign lots for equality. I raise funds for indigenous charities, I attend, and I shake placards, at various rallies and sign petitions. I do lots of grass root, direct-action things and I openly tell my female colleagues how much I earn (and they often laugh and walk away).

This is not me virtue signalling, it is me explaining what my baseline of decent behaviour is.

It just shits me so much, when here in Australia, there are photographs of the current batch of politicians sitting in parliament and it's a smug sea of white male faces smiling out. Ggrrr!! Very few First Nations People and hardly any women, what the fuck is that about? Yet I understand why people don't all rise up and fight for this to change, the world throws distractions at us. It makes false promises and dangles carrots constantly out of arm's length that we build our lives reaching for.

Don't have pay equality? Not a problem, just read this glossy magazine, it'll make you feel stylish, independent and sexy and take your mind off all that unpleasant inequality thingy ...

Angry about the incarceration rates of indigenous teenagers, shocking isn't it, you should be, but here, lets address the pressing issues around climate change (although nothing changes) BEFORE we get to that....

At the end of your wits about the numbers surrounding deaths of women by domestic violence, look it is dreadful, but hold on, the Prime Minister (either ours or another country's) is going to say or do something very controversial and/or silly and we should all be paying attention to that tomfoolery instead!

It's all so very fucked! Fucked, fucked, fucked I tell you!

Politics is fucked.

I struggle because I want to fix this issue, however it's so much bigger than I singularly ever will be able to really effect. I can protest, sign petitions and join direct-action groups, but the bad men in power always seem to win. So I do what I can do. I make art. Possibly bad art, possibly the fair few shit paintings I mentioned earlier, but still I make it. I make it because I think I have my ethical baseline covered, but I know it's not enough.

I make art because if I didn't I'd go mad(der).

I make art because I have something to say and not everyone who has something to say is in the position of privilege that I am.

I make art because I like the idea of starting conversations.

I make art because if I show I can, then maybe you too will make art and maybe yours will be THE magical, amazing art the world is waiting for to shake it out of its stupor! (no pressure though, but can you please?)

I make art because it helps me sleep with a brain not on a roller coaster of ideas, anger and whimsy.

I make art because it allows me to think I am somehow contributing to un-fucking the world around me.

That is why I do what I do. Why do you do what you do?

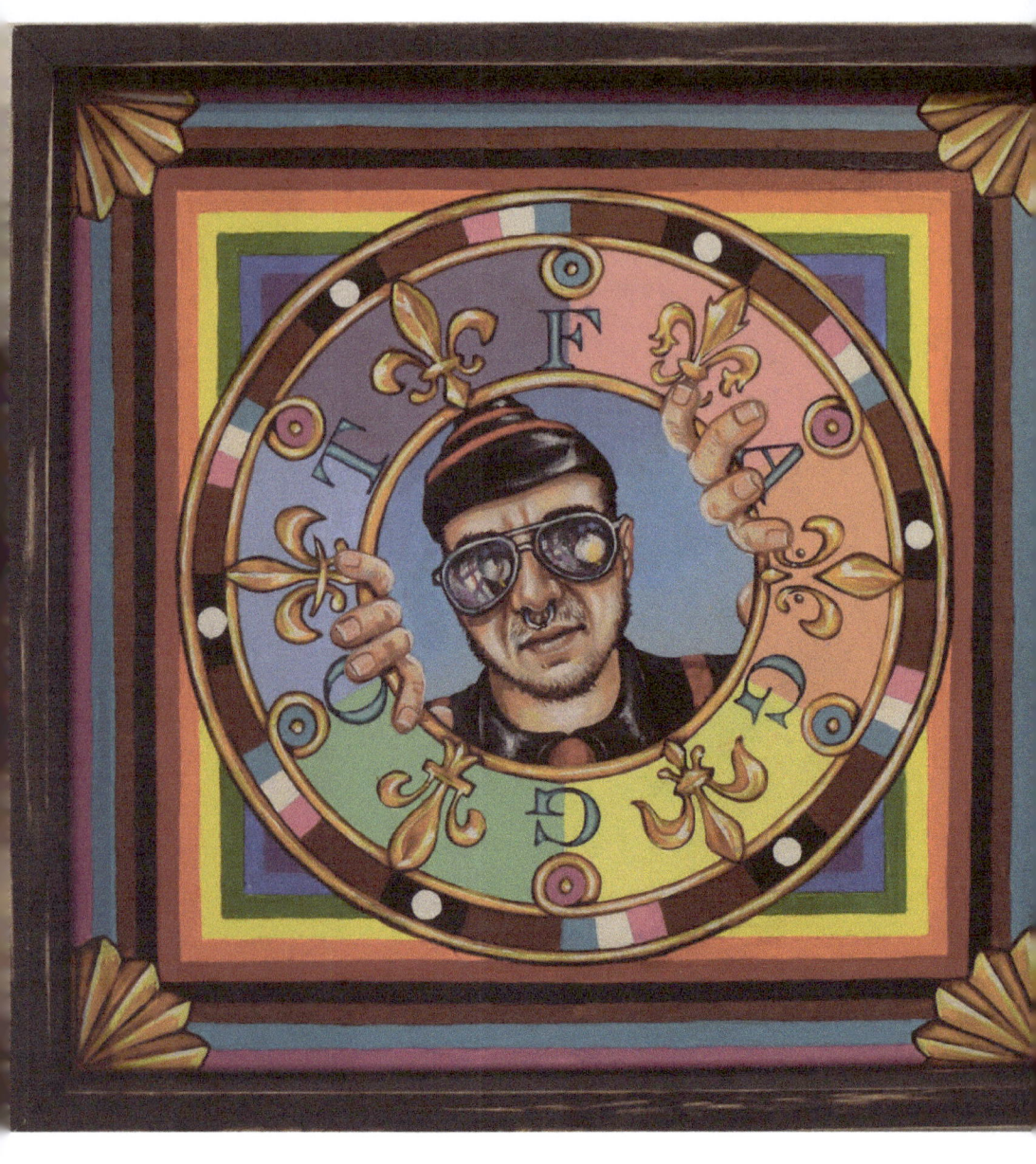

QUEER
QUEER
QUEER

The Urban Dictionary definition of Queer; 'something that is odd, different, strange or non-mainstream.' This is a portrait of my friend Zoo; only it kind of isn't, because a true portrait should really tell you a lot about the person in the portrait. This doesn't really give much away about Zoo, apart from really stating clearly the person in this portrait is obviously very queer. I love making queer and unapologetically queer artwork. Zoo, like myself, embraces their queerdom as a strength (if not a superpower). This artwork actually has a few titles, the one I went with while exhibiting the work was 'Coming to get ya', which, I think adds to the menacing element of the piece.

I never really tell people I'm gay (as if I'd ever need to). Don't misunderstand, its not that I'm ashamed of my sexuality or in any kind of closet, Jesus Beverly Christ, I don't think there'd ever be a closet big enough to contain me or my dress up bags. I'm out and I'm proud and I'm extra loud! I just don't identify as being gay, it's not a description I often use for myself. I prefer the word Queer.

Queer. Queer. Queer.

I prefer being Queer to being gay. Queer is such a good word. I love it. Queer. Even the sound of it provokes naughty, slightly subversive, fun thoughts. Queerdom to me is alternative, compassionate and questioning.

My name is Guy James Whitworth and I am Queer.

I am Queer and proud of it. My taste in music and clothes is Queer, my politics is Queer, my aesthetic is Queer (indeed, I even had an exhibition a few years ago called A Queer Aesthetic) and most of my friends are Queer. Even my friends who are not same-sex attracted are mostly Queer, they manifest their Queerness in other ways and with other ideals, creativity, community connections, and empathy. There's an obvious argument that says you can only claim to use the word Queer if you have been oppressed at some point, but realistically, if you do reach out to use that word as self-identifying, there's a very good chance you have encountered oppression in some form, nowadays who honestly hasn't, also, straight cis frat boys don't usually choose to use it for some reason (although, methinks they might protest too much…).

Queer still has the power to be such a visceral and disturbing word.

Queer. Queer. Queer.

It gets even more powerful when used as an insult, However, watch out, because, more often than not, the power is transferred stylishly to the 'insultee'. Feel free to shout the word Queer at me from your moving car, building site, or lonesome street corner, I'll wave, blow a kiss and flash you my hairy little man titties if you're lucky. But if you think your insulting me, then you have lots to learn. When drawing attention to my Queerness you magically compound it and strengthen it, you highlight it and draw me into the spotlight. It is coals thrown onto the fires within me. Over years the pressure and intense weight applied to us Queers has made us as hard and shiny as the most beautiful diamonds. And you can't cut us with your damp-rag soft insults or pathetic plastic-fork put downs. We are harder formed, precious and more fabulous than our oppressors ever could be. Queer means being me; it means being whatever I want and without having to justify that to anyone else. That you would try to use that word to shame or tame me reveals your naivety, softness and inexperience in the world.

Indeed, there's nowt as Queer as folk, and them folk are my idea of a good time.

I love being Queer, I want to live it, I want to paint it, I want to portray it, I want to define it, I want to embrace it and I want to fuck it as much as I can. In most big cities worldwide there is an underground culture of Queerness and whilst not necessarily universally uniform, it is constant in its localized alternativeness and fierce fabuloulosity! I see it as an intentionally problematic defiance to all things traditional, colonial and establishment. Whenever I travel, straight away I look for the local expression of Queerness, as if searching out a bolt hole in times of trouble.

Queer. Queer. Queer.

Queer is not aware of skin tone, it shrugs and looks past gender, it cares nothing for body shape, it is not exclusionary, or dependent on physical ability, it beckons forward the neurodiverse, and it certainly doesn't waste time counting years. If anything, it is oblivious to all these things. It is all-encompassing and all-inclusive.

Being Queer is a colour palette, it is a thought process, it is a statement, it is a riot, it is revolution, it is a protest, it is activism, and it is political because who I want to fuck and who I need to fight is political. I am never alone in my Queerdom, but I am always unique in my Queerdom. There are many of us, and none of us, individually and collectively, worry about whether or not you approve of the word, the lifestyle, or of us. We are collectively Queer, Queer, Queer.

I state all of this not as an exclusionary statement or a claim to elitism, but as a battle cry and a call out for all who would join us. Come and join our Queer collective. We are on the march, our flags are fabulous and flying high and our numbers are growing. Whoever you choose to sleep with is your concern, but how you decide to interact with the world affects everyone around you. Come to the Queer-side, whether as an ally, an associate an activist, a fan or occasional fuck-buddy, come embrace what it means to be Queer, open up to alternative views, appreciate aesthetics different from your own, consider compassionate ways of solving problems, appreciate colours, question authorities; discover your Queerdom and roll around naked in Queerness like it's glitter on the ground of a parade route and you are freshly damp with kisses!

Join me in my aesthetic, join in my world, join me in my chant. Queer. Queer. Queer.

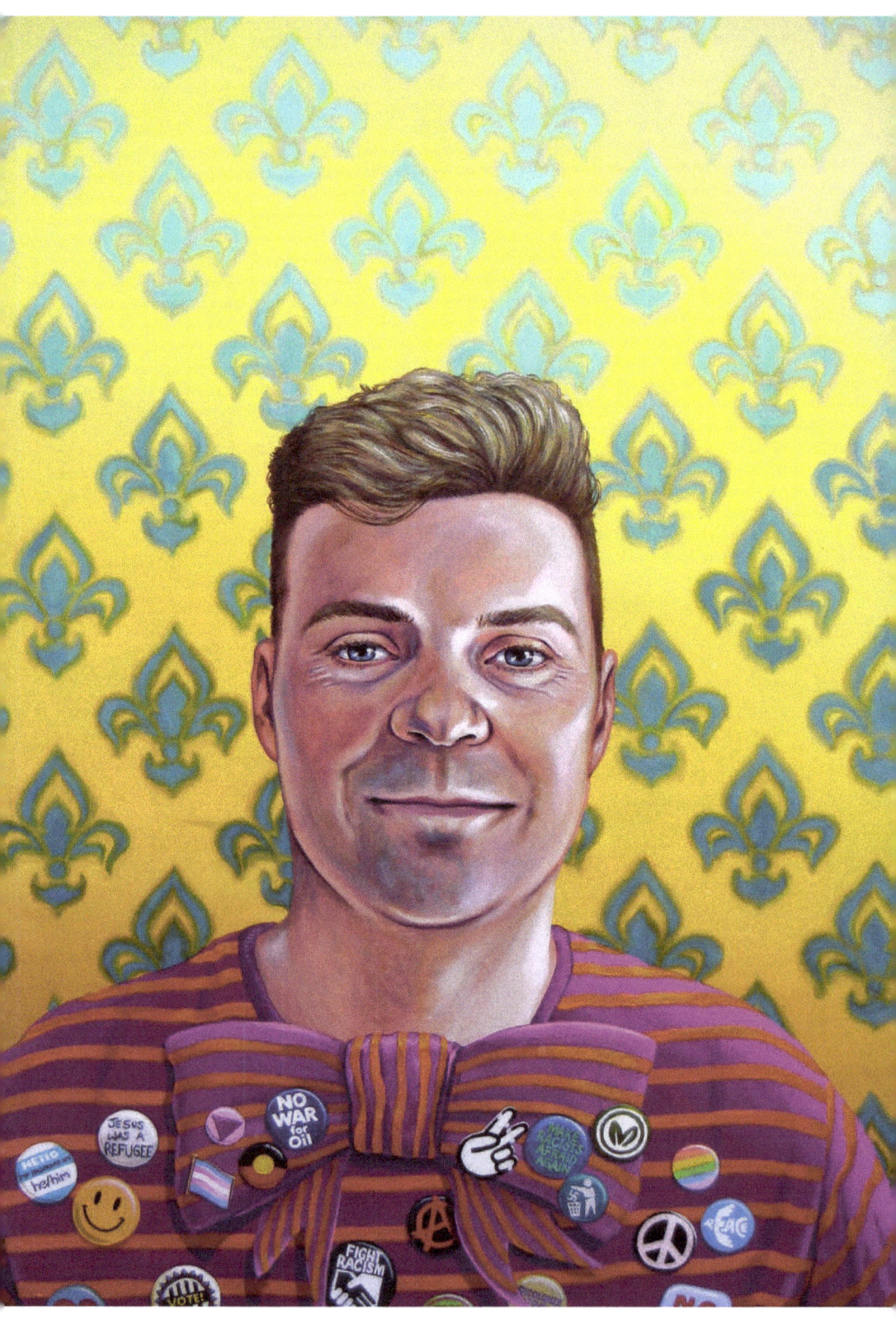

ISN'T FAME A FUNNY OLD SAUSAGE

OR, THE WEIGHT OF EXPECTATIONS

A couple of years ago I was in a café and I placed a coffee order to go (look, it was actually a chai latte with almond milk actually, but don't distract me, there's a lot to get through) and the barista asked if I was an artist; he said he'd seen some of my work and liked it. When it came time to pay, he gave me a wink and said it was on the house. He was a tad flirty and utterly adorable. I thanked him, coyly smiled back and teasingly looked him in the eye and said 'see you again soon' as I left. I live less than 2 minutes' walk from that café and I've never been back there since.

I don't always mind attention and I can confidently, if need be, exercise control over a crowd and comfortably play to an audience if I'm in the mood. I'm good at reading a room and a few different times have spoken in front of rather large crowds with primarily positive results. I'm mostly okay with being recognised as the person I present to the world.

However, I always feel a little uneasy when I'm introduced to someone I don't know who already knows lots about me. That's kind of problematic, I know, since I choose to put so much of myself out into the abyss that is modern online culture.

There is an annual portrait competition each year here in Sydney called The Archibald, and the winning artist gets a meat tray and a magical talking hat, or some such thing. I wouldn't really know what the winner gets to be honest, because despite my best efforts I've never gotten anywhere near being selected as a finalist.

This is a painting of a quite famous comedian I like called Tom Ballard. I emailed his agent and asked if Tom would be up for sitting for me for The Archibald and a few days later Tom called and said he'd love to have his portrait painted by me. He said he had seen my work and liked it. Wow, Tom knew who I was. Wow. Yup, again, even that makes me oddly uneasy.

I like Tom and his sense of humour, and his belief system isn't too dissimilar to mine. He supports the same ideals and often uses his platform to promote those ideals and causes. The point of the painting was to show a fabulous person, unapologetically queer, in a ridiculous, fabulous pink tie neck blouse, with the camp bow weighed down by the burden of too many social causes represented, in this instance, by the badges and buttons. I kind of feel like that some days, as if my fabulousness is weighed down by heavy purpose, although you'd have to ask Tom directly if he does, I'm thinking maybe he might. The finished visual isn't exactly what I had planned, the badges are too evenly distributed, and the bow doesn't flop as dramatically as I'd prefer, but I'm mostly happy with it.

On the day that Tom came to my studio we chatted a little bit about fame and what that word meant. Whilst obviously, he, being a household name, knew more about it than I did, I felt I still made a few quality points of interest. We chatted about how, when I was in my late teens and early twenties (during the 1940s Tom kindly enquired …) there hadn't been any internet or mobile phones (it was actually the late 80s early 90s and I made a mental note to add 20 kilos to Tom's portrait) and how that meant fame was a thing that could, relatively, be controlled and managed. Back then it was a more innocent time with limited media. The tabloid press had recently coined the phrase 'It Girl' to describe pretty young women who were always seen at the right parties and wore the right clothes. Well, I like to think of myself at this time as being one of the first 'It Gays'. I too, was out about most nights, making the most of what London's party scene had to offer. I was reasonably attractive, extremely slutty, and slightly mentally unwell, and as I'm sure we can all agree, this is usually a reliable recipe for infamy and extreme popularity.

I have never actively in my life pursued fame. I do sometimes enjoy attention and I often sashay around the edges of infamy, (Infamy, Infamy, they've allll got it infamy) but fame for fames sake never really appealed, not even back in the late eighties when, at eighteen years of age I first got to London as dumb as a bag of the shiniest dumb buttons you ever did meet.

As part of the fashion course I'd enrolled in, we had to spend a few weeks out of college on 'work experience'. Most students got assigned to some fast fashion factory out in the burbs making coffee and hand stitching skirt hems, but I was way too shallow and pretentious for that. I decided to strike out and ask some of the cool kids I'd started to make friends with out in the clubs if anybody had any contacts in the upper ends of the fashion world. Bearing in mind this is over 30 years ago now, I'm not even going to try to remember too many names, but I'll throw out a couple to add credence to my tale; somehow I was given the direct number to Nicola Jeal, who at that time was the Fashion editor at *The Observer*. I remember making the call from a telephone box just outside of Brixton Tube Station and I couldn't really hear a word Nicola said, but I was mostly sure she'd agreed to see me the following week. Anyway I'd misheard, or my understanding of the situation was all wrong and I turned up at *The Observer* Building in Battersea ready for work on some random day when they absolutely weren't expecting me. Long story short; Nicola took pity on me/saw a chance for some quality entertainment/couldn't remember the number to call security and allowed me to stay for a few weeks as the 'junior Men's assistant fashion writer'.

I later found out Nicola had been called whist she was in a different department of the newspaper and been told by security, 'there's a young man 'dressed as a dancer' wandering around the building and we're guessing he might be here to see you.'.

I loved my brief time there; I ended up staying a few months working off and on (sometimes even paid, although mostly not) when I could be bothered to turn up. Again, it was a time before mobile phones, so getting hold of me must have been a nightmare. As well as basic duties organising the more easy parts of fashion shoots and, running around town being fabulous, meeting designers and seeing collections, I was given the job of clearing out the Samples Cupboard; a huge walk in wardrobe filled with designer samples, well let me tell you, I cleaned it out alright! I was supposed to send every garment back to the PR company or designer that had lent it, but well, since I was the one answering the phone, it was easy to say items had been lost or ruined and as it was *The Observer*, which had a massive national readership, no one was going to argue. It's worth pointing out that then, quite like now, the gendering of clothes meant very little to me and since, at that time, I could fit into most woman's sample sizes, there was certainly no need for me to worry about gender appropriate attire as such. I remember there was delightful pair of culottes that were particularly kicky, swishy and never went without comment, especially when coupled with my old school jumper, riddled with holes, and my favourite platform shoes at the time that looked like little round bubble cars! Fabulous!

Gradually I got known by the great and good of the fashion industry at the time, and I got a phone call one day asking if I wanted some part time work at Lynne Franks, which was the hottest of the hot fashion PR Companies at the time. Yeah, I replied, I suppose I could try to fit it in …

I never really went back to college; I still have no idea if I graduated or earnt a qualification. Odd-jobbing and inappropriately dressing throughout the fashion industry seemed to be far more informative and fun.

At this time, it was a funny phase in London's style history. New romantic was becoming old (floppy brimmed) hat and Rave culture was beginning to raise its hands in the air, like it just didn't care. As with pretty much most style revolutions, youth and beauty were the prerequisite, and I just happened to be young and, well, not quite beautiful, but reasonably okay from a distance in photographs, and at the right time and the right place.

Now London is a big place and there are many different hip and happening scenes that happen at any given time. The gay scene at that time was just beginning to deal with the AIDS crisis and whilst the clubs certainly weren't empty, they were mostly full of the cautious and concerned. No matter to me, or so I believed, I was young and healthy and while AIDS was a definite worry, it wasn't going to stop me going out and enjoying myself as safely as I could. I had been entrusted with a 'media pass' that I used (way longer and more casually than I should) with my name and title at *The Observer* boldly printed on it, and I very quickly worked out that flashing that card got me, and usually a few eminent hangers-on, into most clubs free of charge. No matter that I was a junior, junior, junior fashion assistant, I still worked in fashion! What with 'free' designer clothes, quality contacts, youth, beauty, a love of alcohol and an absolute lack of common sense, I found London's club land was mine, and my mates, for the claiming.

There was a term thrown around at the time; 'Club Royalty' and whist I wasn't actually a crowned head, I was certainly in the court and claiming attention. Legendary fashion designer Jean Paul Gaultier was launching his 'Junior' range of clothing via Lynne Franks and there were many perks to being involved with that particular scene. The 'Look' I had was ridiculous and also ridiculously in fashion. Striped T-shirts, bald head, drawn on dark eyebrows, clumpy and impractical shoes that I constantly fell over in, (as if anyone could really believe me to be a professional dancer!) this was my time to shine and, whenever upright, shine I, kind of, did. Of course, none of this was a natural state of existence for me, and it was bloody hard work to keep the facade of fabulousness up, but I worked hard at it and I was compellingly, naturally, artificial enough to be convincing.

I luckily had a good group of friends just as hopelessly magnificent as I was. Beverly who looked a lot like (a solidly built, Scottish version of) Linda Evangelista; Gary, who was the prettiest, prettiest blonde twink you ever did see; Roger, my amazing designer friend (darling, we should all have one); Mary, who's stage name was Dr Bikini (well, it was until she fell pregnant) ... the list of my dearly beloved hangers on, goes on. Fuck, looking back, we really were tremendous.

In order to make money a few of my friends and I covertly worked on telephone sex lines. The owner of that company asked me if I had any photos he could use for advertising the lines and I sold him a couple of shirtless shots that Beverly took of me (in our tiny bedroom in quite shocking lighting that we thought looked 'edgy') and they were printed in the weekly free gay newspapers of that time. I was easily recognisable in the photos and, not that my ego needed it, I suddenly became even more popular and, even if I say so myself, slightly more fuckable (although just as fucked up) to anyone impressed by such easy infamy.

I went out most nights, very rarely with more than just a few pounds in my pocket (how crude being expected to pay for one's own drinks! Urgh, common!). Everything, well, when I wasn't falling over, seemed to be falling at my feet. I was here, I was queer, I was connected, I was fabulous, I was fashionable and nothing could stop my glamorous rise to glory, infamy and Club Royalty.

However.

Sadly, at the same time as all of this, my mother, who had been battling cancer for the past few years started losing that battle. I was living between exhilarating highs and excruciatingly painful lows almost daily. When days were up, they were really up (such as sashaying around Liberty, the posh London Store, picking out jewellery to be used in a Moroccan themed fashion shoot as perky store assistants ran behind me bundling up whatever I languidly pointed at); and when they were down they were down (sitting outside a hospital ward wanting to cry whilst being growled at by my father (who wasn't dealing well with my mother's illness at all), because I looked too alternative and queer for the local hospital. ('For the fucking love of god, are you wearing women's culottes'?).

Down South in London everything was superficially spectacular; up North, everything was painfully falling apart. Ups and downs. Ins and outs. Swings and roundabouts. Air kisses and emotional kicks in the gut. This went on for a few years, pretty much most of my early twenties and it didn't really do good things for my mental health. Put quite simply, I wasn't equipped to cope. I just didn't have the life experiences or coping mechanisms to process it all. I suppose not many would at that age. It seemed directly related; the more fabulous I became, the more my Mum's terminal cancer spread. I was heartbroken with the prospect of losing her, but I was also heartbroken that I couldn't seem to hang on to the life I was creating and also be a part of her final time.

I had zero money. I shared a bed with Beverly and Gary in a rented room Beverly's mum paid for in shared house in Clapham North. If I wasn't working on the phone lines I would sleep during the day when Beverly was out at St Martins studying fashion and head out most nights, when she'd take her turn and slip straight into the warm spot. I also got a job in a pub in the evening to bring in some money as the phone line work was really taking me to a mindset I knew wasn't healthy for me, but I was utterly unreliable at the pub too, so hardly got any shifts. Every other week I would board a Newcastle bound train from Kings Cross without a ticket and sit in the toilet the entire way (4 hours) and bolt out of the bathroom onto the platform at Newcastle to be greeted by distressed family, always checking behind me for ticket inspectors. This was nerve wracking, but after a while it became the norm. I spent a lot of time alone thinking things through and reading books in train toilets during this time. Who says therapy has to be expensive?

It was an insane time, and I was slowly going insane. I couldn't keep the momentum of it all up and due to travelling backwards and forwards and spinning too many totally different plates. Unsurprisingly, things started to crash down around me.

There was an unfortunate culmination of this insanity one night in London when a good group of friends and I went out to a club called The Daisy Chain at The Fridge (because it's cool, geddit?) in Brixton. It was London Fashion Week and a design company I was working for (when I could be bothered) had just had a super successful catwalk show, so I'd managed to rob a few bottles of champagne which I glugged from heavily after coming off the phone to my parents. My Mum had just had a particularly grim session during a radiation treatment and I told a friend about it at our house before going out (to be honest, getting ready to go out was always the best bit. Was then and still is!). Anyway, that friend, bless him, with no malicious intent I'm sure, went around the whole club telling everyone how ill my Mum was. So of course all night, just after my drugs had kicked in (not paid for by me obviously, but wilfully taken to obliterate what I was truly feeling all the same) all of the people who knew me at that club, and there were so many there was almost a queue forming, kept coming up to me and telling me how sorry they were to hear about how my Mum didn't have long left.

It was awful and I felt truly horrible. Surely I was the worst son in the world. I was here with all of these people in this club and she was in and out of hospital suffering in the worst possible way.

There was a toilet at the Fridge, (upstairs women's toilet on the left hand side for those who want to know) where the lightbulb would often be screwed out and this dim dark, dodgy room turned into a bit of a backroom and men would meet there for sex. I remember on this occasion, once the 'well-wishers' had proven too much for me, pushing through the dark sweaty mass with tears streaming down my perfectly made-up face, sitting in a pitch black cubicle and sobbing my shallow little heart out while the pounding disco beats and squishy sounds of sex echoed around me. Every now and then someone would stop and say they could hear crying, but then the noises and sex would resume and my sobs continued undisturbed in the booming dance music.

Eventually I left the club, pushing through the crowd, with eye makeup running down my face, a drugged up mess and feeling very exposed, like I was that night's grotesque entertainment for the other clubbers.

After that I started occasionally wandering around the streets of South London at night rather than go out clubbing. I'd meander by myself. Thinking and taking in the city. Around this time I also met a very special gentleman caller called Stefan, but more about him coming up soon. I was still frequently blissfully happy, yet just as often, intensely miserable. It was a lot to deal with at a young age and I knew I could get through it, but I also knew I couldn't get through it with an audience. I was fine with people knowing me, but I didn't want people knowing too much about me or having to be publicly accountable for where my head was at.

Which, of course, is ironic that I'm now writing all of this down knowing full well that people will read it and know all of this about me. Irony much? Why, thank you, thought you'd never ask.

I'm older now and I have a thicker skin, understand the benefits of waterproof mascara and enjoy better coping mechanisms. That said, I envy people who can put everything out into the world and not worry about it. I think younger people who grew up with Social Media in their lives from an early age get to do that more easily. I don't mind being observed, but I also like to move in the world unnoticed when I choose to. Fame isn't going to do my sanity any favours, however I have things I want to say, not so much these tales of my drunken youth, but other things; wisdoms I have learnt and points I want to make, so the trade-off with infamy is necessary, and well, a little smidgen of fame and free chai lattes are something I can cope with, just about.

I didn't mind getting the free chai latte because the barista knew who I was. I minded his expectations and I worried about who he expected me to be by just knowing me through my work.

I envy people like Tom Ballard who manage to make their living out of being authentically and consistently themselves and can take fame in their stride whilst incorporating ethics and social awareness into the mix. Very well done them, however, that's not quite me. I'm all over the shop, and I am rarely consistent in my views or wants, and also I stress way too much about 'letting people down' when they meet me.

My Mum passed away a few years after the time I mention above, and I grew up considerably with her passing. That's not to say I stopped going clubbing, stopped abusing my media pass (I have a vague drunken recollection of it shamefully being taken off me at some point) or learnt all of life's lessons at that point overnight. Even now, three decades later, I still have lots to learn and my changing, evolving views are partly part of why I worry about making bold statements in public. I never get into clubs free now, but I do get invited to speak at conferences, write books, mentor younger artists and it makes me mostly happy when people tell me they like my work.

I guess that's how it goes, you get to trade culottes for common sense and media passes for self-understanding. Well, maybe if, in hindsight, you're one of the lucky ones.

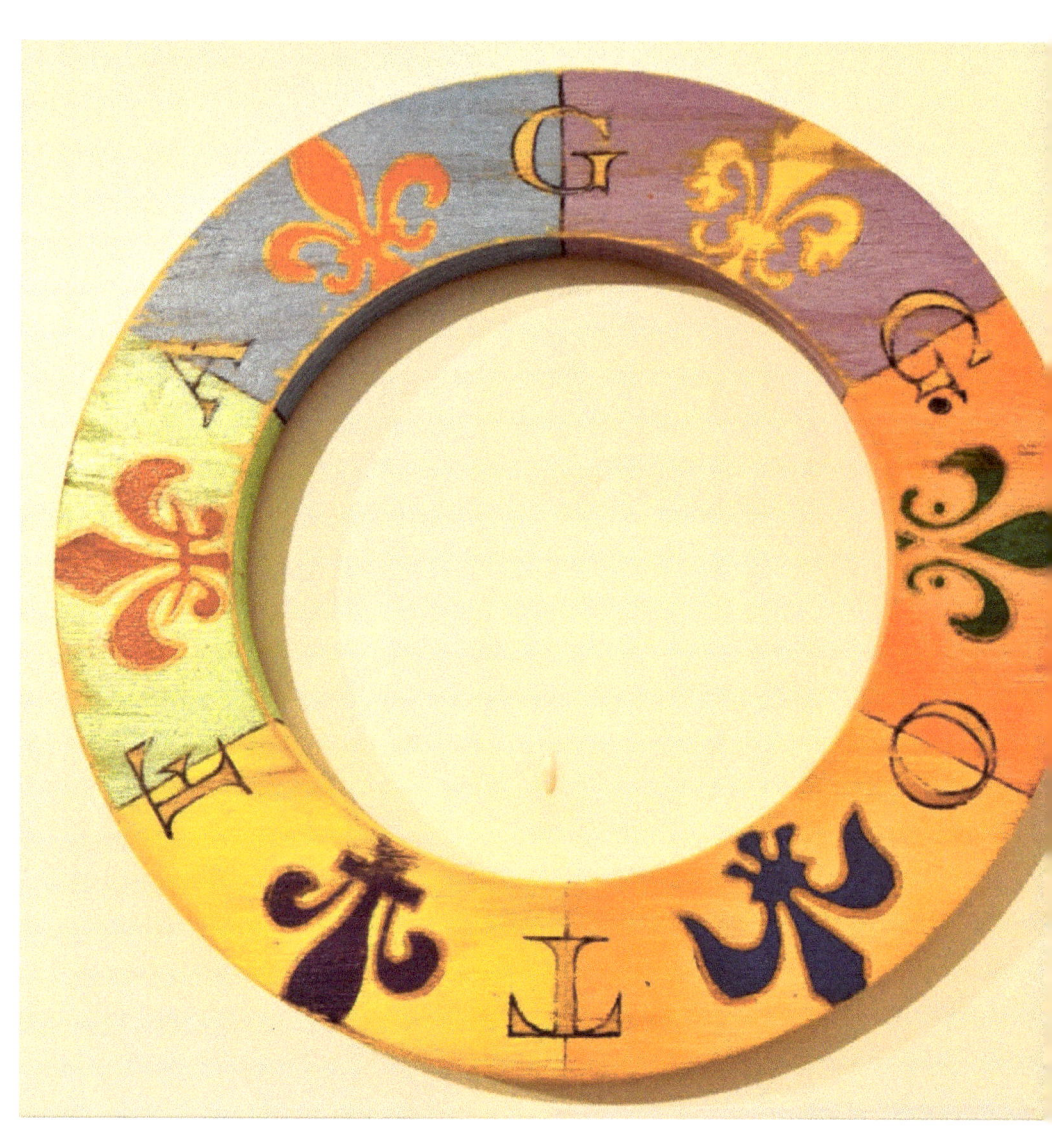

WHAT DID YOU JUST CALL ME?

This is a piece I worked on over lockdown from COVID-19. I have called it 'What did you just call me?'

If you find the word faggot distasteful, then there is a very good chance I didn't make this piece for you.

Bizarrely, when I'm struggling and when I need to get through something, I just allow myself to dwell on my childhood, and you know what, I get encouragement knowing that if I was strong enough to get through that hideous fucking dumpster fire of a time, then I'm certainly now strong enough to get through anything. The lockdown we all had to endure because of COVID-19 was rough, but it wasn't the roughest thing I've ever had to go through, not even nearly.

My childhood was elaborately shit. It was the shit storm of all shit storms. I had an overly thumpy and distant father and was systematically bullied throughout my childhood whenever I stepped out of the house. I literally didn't have a safe space to turn to.

I had quite a few nicknames at school, they tended to change and evolve throughout my pre-teen and teenage years, they ranged in their intended viciousness, but faggot was a continual beauty that was a relentless companion throughout my formative years.

These are some highlights of my other nicknames:

- Poof/poofta (like, d'uh!)
- Faggot (I've actually grown to, kind of, love this word. To me it contains much of what I'm about and what drives me.

- Spick (apparently, I looked Hispanic, I never really hated this one I liked the idea of being different in background to the pastey white dullards who were my bullies)
- Yeti (I was the first boy in my year to reach puberty, so, well, Urgh, I mean yeah, that one maybe makes a little bit of sense)
- Gay-Guy (massive amounts of imagination needed for that one, hi-five kids, awesome job)

So, not surprisingly and certainly not unrelated to what I'm explaining here, I was a very quiet child and dreadfully underconfident. I had a big mop of wavy brown hair (which I suppose encouraged the Hispanic thing) that I would pull down over my face and I'd hide myself away and shrink back from people as much as was possible.

Faggot. It's actually quite a nice sounding word, it rolls well off the tongue. As I discussed in a previous chapter, I have a thing about certain words. I use faggot now affectionately with a few of my friends every now and then, it has no loaded power in those circles, but taken out of those safe situations it can still do damage quite savagely.

I always had dodgy teeth. Too many gaps, which is quite unfixable without very expensive dentistry an artist certainly cannot afford. I've since grown to not mind my gappy teeth, however in the school yard I once heard somebody say about me that I 'could eat an apple through a tennis racquet' which to be honest still to this day makes me chuckle, but obviously, again, at the time, certainly didn't help my confidence levels and I remember fighting back tears. A continual shout in the playground was 'backs against the wall' whenever I walked past or around a crowd. This was to me strangely potently hurtful and it was only years later that I worked out why. It implies that I am somehow about to assault or sexually attack, which as a child that suffered great physical abuse, was particularly hurtful as it implied, to me in my young mind, I was wilfully passing on that trauma.

My home life was really spent waiting for and trying stressfully to avoid physical abuse from my violent father. He was an ex-military man and someone who wasn't unaccustomed to using his fists to get a point across. Often the violence isn't as bad as the ongoing fear of violence and after a while the pain from a punch or kick will fade, but then the fear of the next punch or kick replaces it and that takes its toll for a very long time.

As quick as I could, I left school at sweet sixteen and went running off to study fashion at Art College. Unfortunately, I wasn't the only thing making a break for it and I was diagnosed with male patterned baldness three months after my sixteenth birthday and my hairline started receding with vicious enthusiasm. Yup, even mother nature decided to have a dig. Fucker.

There are pictures of me at seventeen playing with my newborn nephew and I look old enough to be his grandparent. Two lovely little hyphenated words for you; comb-over. Let's just leave that there. You live, you learn, you clipper.

Just when I thought I understood what under-confidence was, I discovered new depths. But you see this was part of the making of me. From eighteen onwards I have always shaved my head, I like to think it works for me and it's 'my thing.' While I certainly have to work harder for it than naturally attractive men with glorious full heads of hair, I certainly have never really struggled with lack of male attention.

At eighteen I left home for the big smoke down south. But as we all know, just because you chose to leave everything behind, it doesn't mean it all doesn't all up and follow you regardless.

I am who I am, and my confidence now ebbs and flows. Some days I can 'bring it'; some days I can't find it to bring, because its wandered off and hidden itself amazingly well amongst my insecurities. But mostly I can get through the day, pretending to be an orderly adult who makes things, paints things and writes about things in an organised way.

In my mid-twenties, one of my friends, who is a fashion designer, had a menswear show at a big London venue. He asked all his male friends to model for him, except for me. Now, realistically I should point out, this upset me for roughly about ten seconds and then I laughed it off. I would have been the shortest person on the catwalk by at least a full foot, and whilst I like to think maybe I could have still carried off the look, it's kind of a relief to never have to find out. So why do I mention it now? Well, honestly, because I'm a dumb, privileged white man and realistically that rejection has still stayed with me in some little way like some tiny abrasive toxic residue. What a pointless waste of energy, yet here it is!

I had a conversation a few years ago with a friend of mine, Candy, after she laughed at my moping around after being rejected for a painting prize. She was a poet and a woman of colour and to quote her, 'you haven't even begun to experience rejection' and she was right; but it's more complex than that. It's not the amount of rejection you can deal with but how you deal with the ongoing rejection that's thrown your way that defines who you are. I let it hit me and affect me, but not permanently shape me.

I get through all of life's current taunts, rejections and insults because I've lived through them all already. I'm not attractive enough? Fine, heard it before, not a problem, I'm too gay? Yup, without a doubt, so best look elsewhere. Oh, you don't like my art? Well fine, go dry finger yourself, because I didn't make it for you!

Some of my art is confrontational and some of it, without it being explained, can appear quite sweet. A few pieces have won awards. But a lot many more pieces haven't. Some of it sells, some of it doesn't. Them's the breaks and that is the awkwardness of making art, and also writing. It can be an unpredictable and bumpy road, however, unpredictable and bumpy roads can still lead to worthwhile destinations. Sometimes there are drunken straight boys standing in the middle of the road shouting faggot. Sometimes there aren't.

Faggot is a word I get to claim and use as I feel fit. And now it is a term that to me means friendship, camaraderie, resilience and a brave queer bundle of fabulousness that just told you to go dry finger yourself. Feel free to remind me of that by shouting it at me whenever you feel fit.

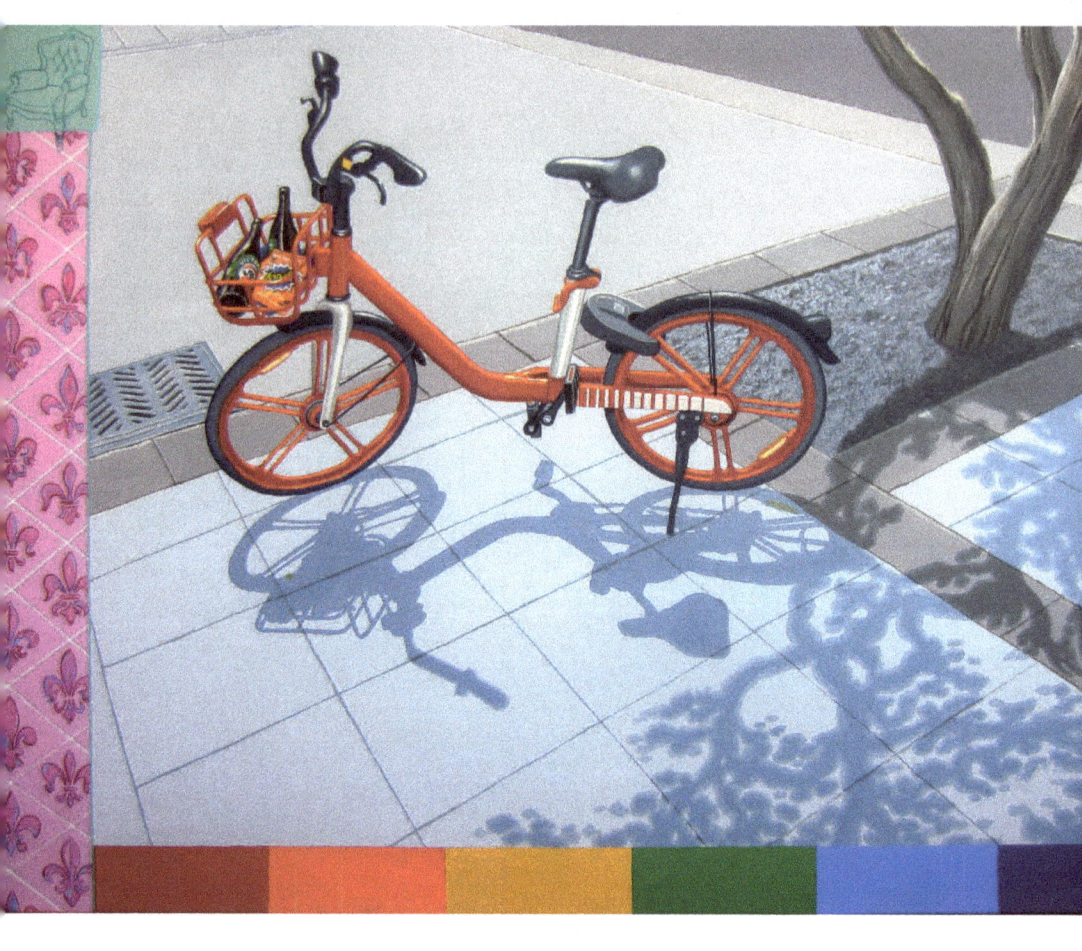

STRAYLIAN SUMMER

Who doesn't love summer? Strong shadows and sun warming our bones. Dappled light and late nights. Warm evenings and loose clothing. I'm very happy to live in Australia but it still challenges me each year with the intense heat of summer that I'm never quite prepared for. I am a short, bald chunky man; I'm fine with that; but short, bald, chunky and dripping in sweat is not a good look. Australian summers are harsh, too harsh, not the gentle green summers of England and northern Europe filled with the long airy dusks of evening and relaxing birdsong.

Early in 2020 we had the crazy month-long bushfires. Fuck. That was a hell on earth no one was prepared for. That can't become the new normal. I don't live anywhere near bushland or open plains so this image to me of isolated, (that word again) desolate, stark shadows was my portraying of this year's dreadful summer.

Smoke filled days and a choking smell of smoke wasn't fun. Obviously others, out of the cities had it much worse. The tales of what life was like out in the country were so upsetting. Australia is an unforgiving country to say the least and we can't let it get any worse through our own mismanagement. Climate change freaks me the fuck out. It is bigger and badder than any of us and we need to act now on fixing what humankind is breaking.

My first ever real love was a man called Stefan, and the year after I moved to Australia, he came to visit. He hated the place. He was dropping by on his way back to London after a three-month stint in India and ironically he found Sydney too crowded, the people here too pushy, and the place too cold (he did visit in the depths of winter). Stefan is really special to me, a bit of a soul mate, although he lives in London, and we rarely chat other than random messaging. He was my first proper relationship and I absolutely, utterly and completely loved him. I think, well, I'm pretty sure I was also his first proper love too (if not his very greatest even, I mean, let's be honest, look at me, I doubt he'll ever do better).

We were together for just under three years. We met in a nightclub queue back in Brixton in the early nineties. I remember I was wearing 'rocking-horse' platform training shoes that I couldn't walk in (i.e. they curved up at the front, so I constantly was in a state of falling or at best staggering forward) and we had a clumsy pash on the dancefloor and then he came back to mine. Who says romance is dead! I literally did fall for him when I first met him, about four or five times as we walked home I believe. Towards the end of our three years, my Mum passed away and I stopped wearing silly shoes (well, mostly) and grew up approximately 100 years.

Stefan is French and had moved to London about a year before I met him. He was originally from a leafy satellite town outside of Clermont Ferrand in le Massif Central of France, I mention this because this to me, at this time, seemed like one of the most glamorous places in the world.

It was all so very, very, what's the word I'm searching for? French—that's it!

He was taller and slimmer than me and a lot more beautiful, but luckily he saw in me what many don't. Also in hindsight, he obviously had low self-esteem at the time, and that worked in my favour. He had those big, soft, plump lips that only French people seem to possess and big brown eyes that could convince me to do anything that I'd probably regret later. He had bleached white hair he'd cut himself, and tattoos that, at that time were still cool and quirky. After he and I had been together a while he started taking me with him to France where we would visit his family and we would stop in Paris en route. This was a big fucking educational thing in my world and literally taught me how to transition into adulthood and being able to look after myself. His being gay didn't seem as big an issue to his family as it was to mine. I don't know if Stefan ever really came out to his family in as much as we were just there, it all seemed fine, and I was welcomed with open arms and kisses on both cheeks. Bonjour, bonjour! Comment cava?

When I first met him he was living in a series of squats, all on the lovely old Victorian terraced streets between Clapham and Brixton in South London. At the time I was often moving from one address to another, so I stayed with him lots in one particular squat just beside Clapham North. I was never actually homeless as such, since I definitely had places to stay, but in hindsight it occurs to me, I certainly wasn't that securely housed either!

The squat would be shared between a few people who all assisted in the 'claiming' of that building as our home. There was about 5 of them from memory and each was a character to say the least, it was an exciting, multicultural and risky way to live and I loved it. The squats would never be safe for too long, what with the fear of nasty men with dogs or bailiffs being sent around from the council bearing eviction notices, but I remember we stayed in this one particular squat for what seemed like most of the summer before we got moved on.

Stefan at the time had acquired a few mice (both shop bought and wild) that we looked after and he rigged up a spectacular 'mouse run' around the upper half of our room of ladders and shelves, tubes and planks of wood around the picture-rail so the mice could run around, feed and live quite happily, looking down on us, but without ever having to come down. Most of the mice had names, but were still very much wild creatures.

At this house he had claimed the downstairs front room and had built something akin to a four-poster bed in the window nook. At the time he and I had a thing for crystals and we would hang them in the big bay window and I have a clear memory of waking up, lying in the bed, wrapped sleepily around Stefan and watching the community of mice run around above us as dappled and multicoloured light from the crystals danced and bounced around the room.

Often in the evening we would precariously climb up onto the sloping roof of the squat looking out over the rooftops of London, with the city skyline in the not so far distance and smoke a lovely herbal cigarette and watch city lights come on and dusk settle whilst chatting to the other housemates and putting the world to rights.

That time was one of true happiness.

Whenever I am asked the question 'when were you happiest?' I can answer straight away; it was around this time, in France, lying on my back in long green grass, drinking beers on a sunny afternoon situated half way up a mountain overlooking the Chaine Des Puys, watching men in hang-gliders jump off the mountain and soar crazily high above us! Freedom, greenery, true love, fresh air and cold beer after big bike rides. Wandering through the streets of Clermont Ferrand was just life at its best, not because I had lots of anything at the time, but just because I was simply happy with my lot and being with Stefan.

I gave up odd jobbing in the world of fashion because, I told people, 'I thought it was shallow and pretentious' but realistically it was because I had a bad reputation and word had gotten around I was thoroughly unreliable. Stefan worked as a life model for artists (he still does and he has a really impressive collection of sketches of him given to him by some really quite established artists) and he got me some work modelling at an art school in Chelsea. We would cycle there together and go smoke joints in Battersea park in our lunch breaks and then back in the studio try not to make each other giggle as we often modelled side by side. Being still for hours at a time is hard. I'd often see students stare past me to take in the beautiful, naturally slim man with the six pack and tattoos, but I'd laugh it off and pull awkward faces or poses for them to have to draw as vengeance. Stefan and I perfected the skill of the silent but deadly fart and would impassively watch the students faces as the smell wafted around the room like some rotten-egg-drenched Mexican wave. I learnt so much from sitting still, trying not to fall asleep and listening to those tutors walk around the classroom to critique and appraise the students work. It was a fabulous, old, charcoal marked place and was exactly the art school I should have really attended as a student. There were both royalty and ruffians in those classrooms and since I never studied art, any formal understanding of art I have was acquired in those chilly, drafty and farty classrooms.

I have always had the theory that artistic talent is not magically gifted by some godlike deity, but it arrives only by hard work and being able to communicate visually so others can understand it. Show me your drawings that you think aren't any good and I'll show you some strong points and exactly which bits you need to practise. I'm yet to have my mind changed. We all have artistic talents, just some of us have spent time working on and perfecting theirs.

I've been to Paris countless times in my life and it is one of my favourite cities in the world. Not so much because of the cliched reasons of its stylishness and grandeur, but quite the opposite, I find it very chilled and relaxed, or at least the bits I go to are. When I'd go there with Stefan we'd stay at the cheapest hotels we could find, try to sneak in all the best galleries without paying and drink black coffees, eat fresh fruit and cheap baguettes when we couldn't afford anything else. I'd been vegetarian since I was a child and with Stefan we kind of just progressed into veganism more often than not, I'm pleased this was the case because although this was my frivolous time of smoking and drinking lots, it was also a time of healthy eating and cycling everywhere, which kept me fit, and set me up for good habits in later years. I tried to learn as much French as I could, and I learnt lots, although I'd often get words completely wrong and make a tit of myself. Still, I had fun doing it (I often confused the word Voiture, which means automobile, with the words Au revoir, which means goodbye, that was always fun as I'd walk out of a café and confusingly shout the word 'automobile' at the bemused waiting staff).

Often Stefan and I would board a coach at Victoria station in London at midnight and wake up the next day in Paris (well, realistically after being woken up at 2 am to get off the bus, walk around a freezing cold ferry sailing across the English channel for two hours and then board the coach again for an uncomfortable morning drive to Paris). Cheap travel can be such a joy around Europe! We would spend as much time there as I could convince Stefan to commit to, although he never liked it there; it was too French for him, and we'd return to London to sign on to claim the dole, model and just generally hang whenever we felt like it. Ah, those glorious pre-Brexit days …

London was amazing fun, we had so little, but experienced such a lot. We would hitchhike to music festivals and jump the fence to get in with no idea about how we'd get home. Life was definitely a bit of a struggle, but we were in such a place of enthusiastic happiness. Stefan, tired of the squatting life, got a proper place to live above a Tandoori Restaurant in Clapham Common, sharing with a Sister of Perpetual Indulgence, and we'd lean out the window smoking joints and giggle at men hanging around the toilets opposite. We often lived off veggies we'd haggle for in Brixton market and then hang around at the end of the day to see what we could salvage from the big skips behind the railway arches where stall holders threw out the vegetables they couldn't sell. There is only one vegetable that I can't eat, and that's okra! After the trauma of eating 'slightly off' okra too many times back then, when it was slimy and slightly fizzy, even the thought of it still now turns my stomach!

Paris for me was never an artistic place, as I could never realistically travel with any art equipment, but occasionally it was somewhere that I'd take time to write, as then, like now, I'd often have a small journal with me. Apropos my artistic theory, writing is a learned skill and anyone can write with practise and a sturdy sense of self. Stefan was incredibly creative but not really the most focused person I've ever met in my life. He and I would come up with grand plans and set out on creative adventures; we made earrings and jewellery out of papier-mache and sold them in local shops, (although we found out later they would turn to mush if they got wet) we would go to the local glass shop and pull out mirrors from their bins out the back and make elegant mirrors with recycled frames (out of anything we could find) and sell them on market stalls. We once attended a Pride march and sold brightly coloured clay badges we'd made declaring 'poof' and 'dyke' (and wondered why people got upset with us!) we were hustlers, but ethical, well meaning, creative and authentic hustlers and we were blissfully happy…

Until.

My mum died and Stefan decided he wanted to go to India.

Now, as tempting as it was to run away, on my list of things to do, India wasn't anywhere near the top, in fact it wasn't even near the bottom because it wasn't on there. I would love to go now, but at the time, nope. At that time in my life I needed, well I'm gonna say 'self-discovery' but really it was just time to grieve and find some kind of purpose in life. I knew India just wasn't going to provide those head spaces or options. I needed to look inward to find myself; Stefan needed to go travelling to see what he could find out in that big world that would entertain or inspire him next. There was no villain of the piece, as is the case with most young love, we just grew in separate directions.

However, now, whenever I smell marijuana being smoked outside or taste bitter black coffee, this is the joyous time my mind drifts back too. I know that I can never have that time again, and that's fine. I actually don't mind the aging process and I am now older than my mother ever got to, so that's something to celebrate. However, I do miss the hazy, crazy, gentle days of summer warmth and of bearable, gentle sunshine.

This year I helped organise an 'Art Auction' with the funds raised going to bushfire victims and to Indigenous Youth Climate charity. We ALL have to do something to help stop the advance of climate destruction. We have no option. I'm fine, I have memories of better times and liveable climates to sustain me, but younger people growing up right now actually don't! The idle joy and summer nights of my youth are something to treasure and we can't deprive people of that carefree living. Do it for the youth but also do it for the short, bald, chunky men who cannot carry being short, bald, chunky and sweaty!

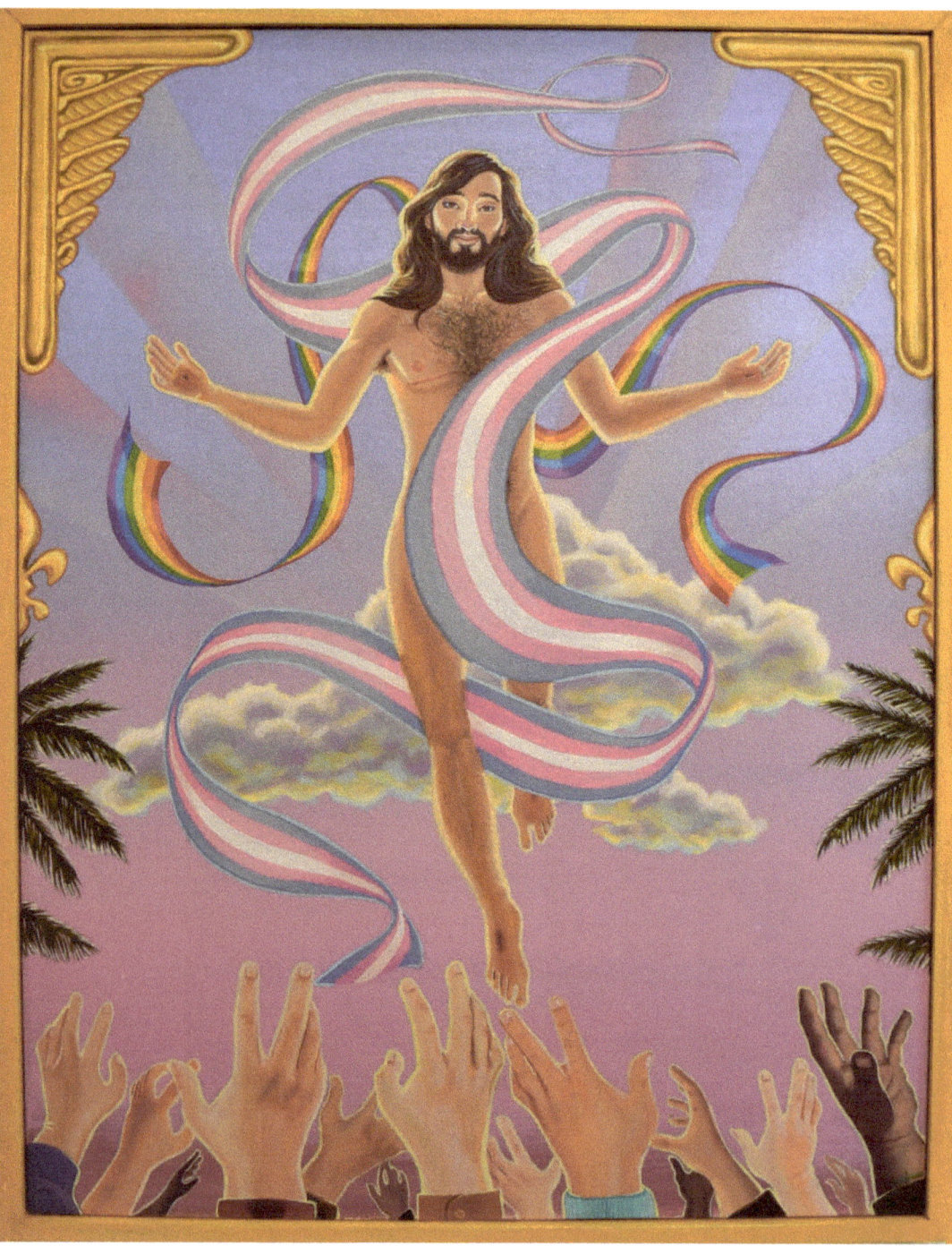

THE ASCENSION OF NON-CIS JESUS

I need to think up a better title for this piece. I like the piece, it's one of my favourite paintings. I often joke that I can't paint hands (best to point it out before anyone else does) but check out that selection of hands bishes!! Oh yeah, this gurl can paint hands! (sometimes)

It took me a few months, off and on, to paint. Too much to think about. I kept planning it out in my mind then backing away from it slightly scared by what I was trying to say. Was what I was saying too controversial? Was it maybe not controversial enough? Was I saying what I was saying just to *be* controversial? Ooh I tell you, I exhausted myself thinking about it all waaaay to much! Once I actually got into it, it kind of just flowed out, so to speak.

Representing a queer Jesus is a constant reoccurring theme in my work. I mean come on, think it through, he had twelve very close male friends and his bestest girly mate was a sex worker. I mean really? Do not even get me started on the lovely smocks with matching sashes he's often portrayed in. There's a saying up North, where I come from, along the lines of 'as queer as a nine-bob note!' Look, I'll be honest, I'm not sure who Bob is, or what needs noting, but I hope you get the point I'm trying to make.

My Jesus is a queer, fem, non-cis Jesus of colour and I don't care what you think. Well actually I strangely do. I want you, the viewer, to think about who Jesus was, wasn't, couldn't have been and what he could still yet come to symbolize if we open our minds!

I have a few queer Jesus paintings in my portfolio and I always struggle with the titles. I did think about calling this piece 'Show me your heavenly body and I'll show you mine', but I feel that's just too much of a *double entendre* even for me.

The colours of the sashes floating around and hiding the blushes of my trans, queer, Jesus of colour are of the LGBTQI and trans flags.

If I was re-doing the painting I'd now include the black and brown that is in the 'Liberation' rainbow flag, that just didn't occur to me last year when I was painting this, but now, I know better and would purposely include them.

I try not to follow other people's paths. I like to do things my own way and in ways that feel right for me. I try not to play the art world's games and I try to avoid the yukky toxically pretentious people from the Sydney Gallery system, it's very narrow minded and very old school in its straight cis-male centric pompousness.

I had a well-known art collector in Sydney make an offer for this picture, but then later back out, I can't help but think it's because they didn't fully understand the title when they made the offer.

I have been told by a few friends who work in Sydney galleries this kind of kitsch representation of religious themes is looked down upon in true artistic circles, but I don't care. This piece has been shared on many Instagram posts online and I have been approached by a fair few trans people to say they love the representation they see in this painting. One young person said they printed it out and have it in their prayer book so when they are in church on a Sunday morning and need support, they can look at it and take encouragement for who they are. And that is worth so much more to me than the acceptance of the Sydney art world.

As I type this, behind me on wall, Non-cis Jesus hangs resplendent in its Queerdom, I love it and I'm happy to keep it for a while, I don't doubt that it will find an appreciative buyer and forever-home at some point soon. And that is fine because it gives me time to think up a better name, but I'll make sure whatever name it ends up with, it's one that still makes straight, ignorant douchebags feel uncomfortable.

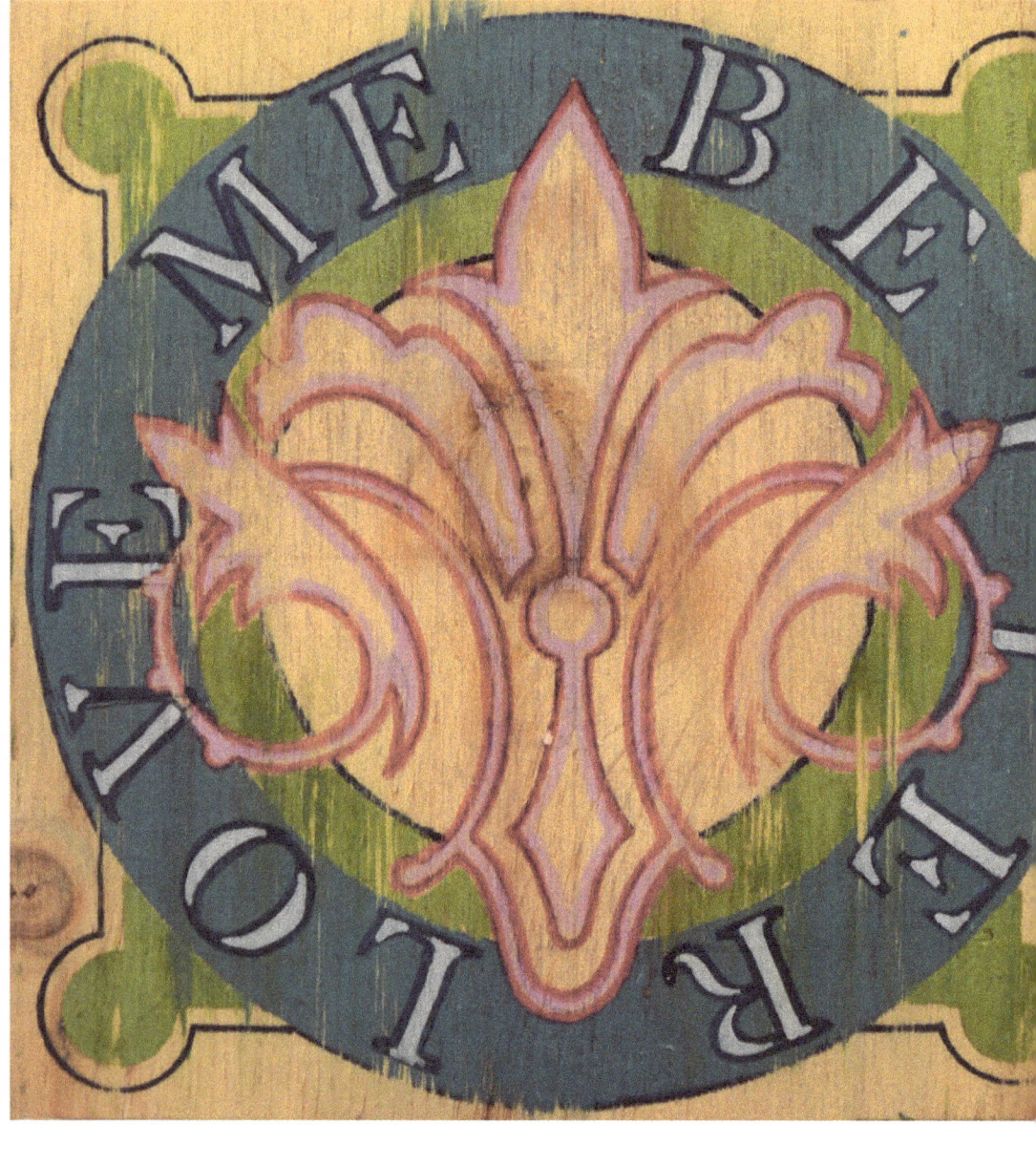

LOVE ME BETTER

Relationships are like a penis, sometimes they're just hard for no known reason.

I know the grass always seems greener and those that are single think being in a relationship would make life so much better/easier/more enjoyable but, yeah, some days I dunno, doesn't matter where the grass is, somebodies still got to tend to it.

I love my partner and couldn't imagine not being with him (I wrote about him lots in my fist book, *Signs of a struggle*. I talk about him releasing his signature scent, not glamorously through a perfumery however, just in the car and not cracking a window) but between him and I we have so many projects and are so time poor. Some days it's hard to negotiate slightly what we both want before the challenges of modern life are added into the mix.

I carry so much emotional baggage; I know I do. Trauma, bad habits, past relationships and bad behaviour learnt from our parents weigh most of us all down, but anyone who reads my writing knows, I've had so many lives and so much experience finding ways to leave all that behind, to be open, gentle and authentic, well, it can all become overwhelming at times.

My parents had a mostly loving relationship, I think, but jeez that said, they enjoyed a good argument! As I spoke about before, my dad was a violent man and more than once I saw scenes of physical violence no child should see. As a child I was often the target of his violence, his anger and his frustration at the world, and those things can alter ongoing behaviour in adults if unchecked.

It's hard, I see so much of him in me, I see pretty much all of him apart from the violence, but I know I still have intense behaviour in some ways, which although different in structure can have the same outcomes of self-harm if left to fester (indeed, not unlike a silent but violent fart in a sealed vehicle).

As with some survivors of abuse I can often blame myself. Was it my obvious queerness as a child that provoked the anger and wrath around me? Throughout my writings, many times, I have written pages that chronicle the bullying and beatings I had from my father, but also outside of the home, in schools and in the area I grew up, but because of guilt and shame I've gone back countless times and deleted those sections and reworded them and covered them up with humorous asides and camp viciousness. I use different forms of humour, such as cattiness and sarcasm, just as I use colour and light to disguise or camouflage the message in what I paint.

I won't lie, some days it's really hard. I know I bring all of this pointless, residual guilt and fault with me now into the relationship I have with my partner, my friends and the world around me and I hate myself for it.

In this piece when I say 'Love me better' I am talking to myself more than anyone else. It is a reminder to myself to make the effort to forgive and allow love to fill that space that forgiveness and kindness creates. Some days I get so frustrated, a violent outburst would make perfect sense! However, I know where I get that from and what outcomes it would bring. I am a work in progress. An artwork that may never be finished (or understandable to anyone else). I'm trying my best, that may not be good enough. But fuck it, I'm going to do my absolute bestest that I can, to make myself a person worthy of love.

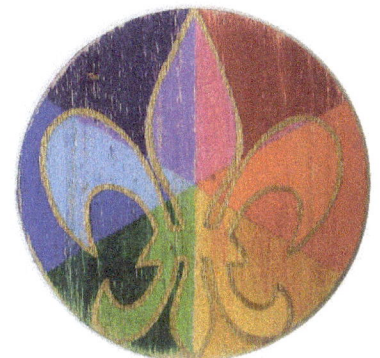

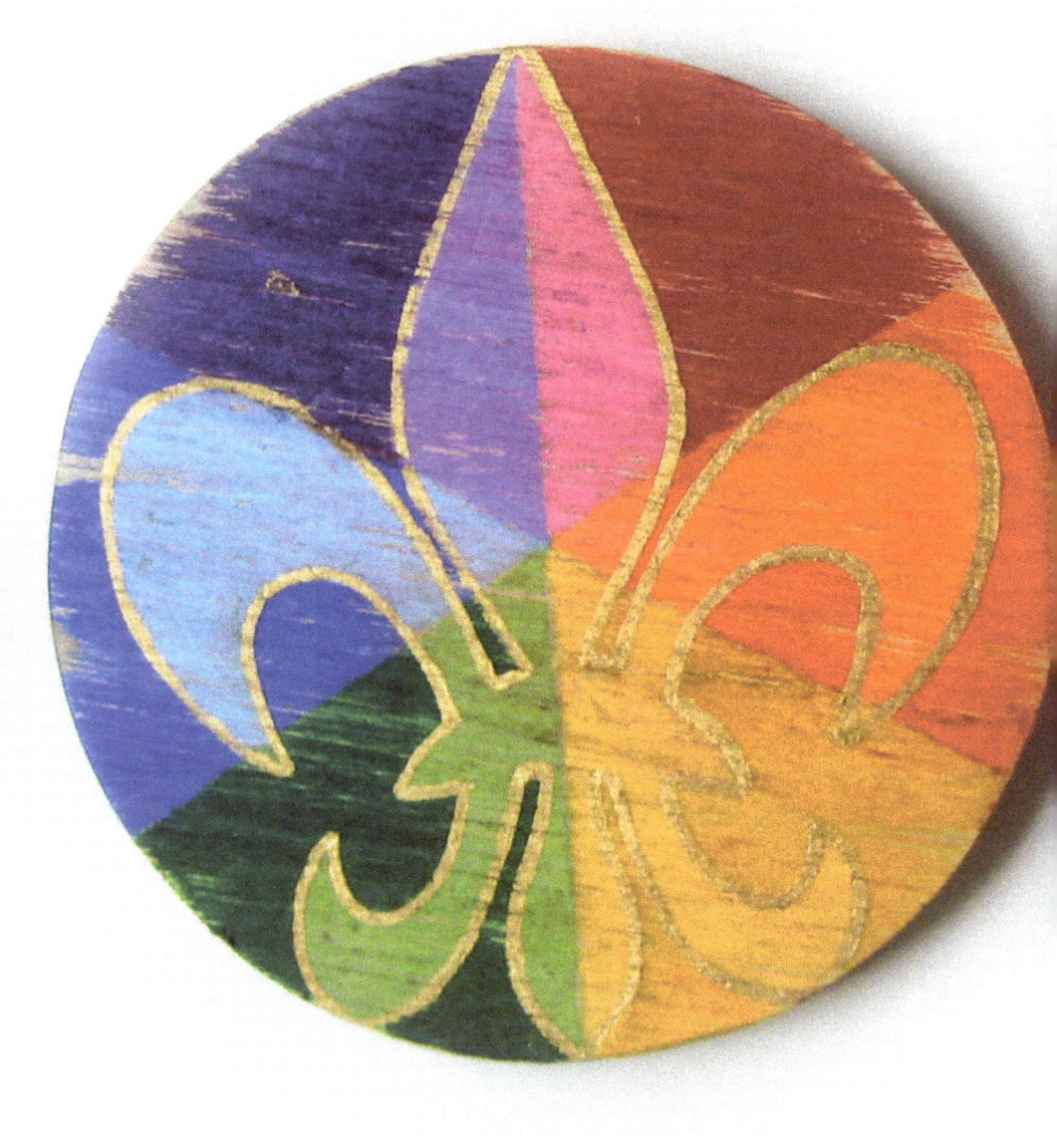

TINY ESSENTIAL VICTORIES

You know those laminated cards in the back pocket of seats on planes you always ignore? Specifically, the illustration that explains you should only help others with the oxygen masks that drop from the ceiling after you've helped yourself? Well let me tell you, them is wise fucking words those.

During the shut-down for COVID19 I struggled. I mean, obviously we all struggled in various ways and various degrees. Jeez, tough audience, but since you are calling me out on it, sure, I probably didn't struggle the most out of everyone I know, but this privileged white child's struggle still felt real enough, nonetheless. A big part of that was everybody telling me what an awesome time this was for artists; all that time to sit indoors and create, they couldn't wait to see all the work I'd produce!

Fuck off fuckers.

The creative part of my brain doesn't really work in that way, and I, burdened by the drama of probable death, society's imminent collapse and the shortage of toilet paper, freaked myself out into an almost artistic standstill and I barely ventured into my studio. My creative urges suddenly felt very stifled under the weight of everyone's expectations. I called this COVIDcreativeblock19

All of a sudden, there was a lot of things that I really needed to watch on Netfilx, Stan and Disney+.

In truth, I felt scared to peel back the seal on my thought process and my mental activity veered erratically between 'WE'RE ALL GONNA DIE' and 'what's the fuckin point? I might just stay in bed' and 'If I could paint hands better this pandemic might never have happened.'

This 'unprecedented' break down of societal structure did fall conveniently into the months just before No Meat May kicked off (an annual challenge I run with my partner Ryan – look it up, it's fun – you get to save the planet by just saying no thankyou to sausage rolls!) so I kind of busied myself with that, thinking up slogans, photographing delicious plant-based food and cobbling together edgy left-of-centre graphics for the campaign. However, it quickly became clear my random, overly enthusiastic but haphazardly thought-through input, wasn't really appreciated by Ryan, so I kind of backed away from that too. This further compounded the 'everything I do is pointless' feeling.

I absentmindedly attempted to paint a portrait (remotely from photographs) of a friend who is a therapist, who, when I rang to offer excuses about why the portrait was taking so long, shared some wise advice with me. She said, 'Maybe the best we are able to do is to just get through this as best we can with as little self-damage as we can', and that wise advice really triggered a slow change of mindset.

I'd unwittingly taken the side of the baying crowd and was expecting too much of myself. Perform monkey, perform! Jeez, surely if anybody should know my lazy-ass-limits it's me! Once I removed (or rather just wandered off and ignored) the pressure I felt from others to create culturally relevant masterpieces on an hourly basis, and blocked out the constant bulletins of badly foreboding news so readily available on social media, I found there was still an indefinable creativity there within me waiting to cautiously peer out and allow its potential to be considered.

That was the end of one struggle and the start of the next. I've never been one to be overawed by the big, blank, white of a bare canvas. I am way too man-confident and uneducated to be intimidated by such thoughts; but I still found myself sluggish and fearful of what possibly dark paths my creative thoughts may lead me down. As is often the case with depression and mental health issues, I found it all just a bit too difficult to get started; every task was too demanding. I had the tools. I had the time. I had the technical abilities, but I could not convince myself there was any worth to it.

So, I started giving myself tiny, fun creative assignments to complete. Scale was the key. Very small and undemanding projects which I could abandon without issue if I decided. I allowed myself more time of just sitting in my studio contemplating things. I chose to paint on objects that were not expensive canvases, but disposable and 'found' items. A few months earlier I had climbed into a skip (don't judge me, I'm an artist darling, I'm an artist!) to rescue some round wood offcuts and I started playing with those. And rather than encouraging myself to think up a large narrative to execute, I chose to let my mind just go wherever it chose in whatever scale it felt comfortable with.

Rainbows: rainbows are easy! These pieces were just small technical tests; could I paint a 50% tonal difference in rainbow range of shades without measuring out the paint? Turns out (mostly, kinda, convincingly) I could. I collectively christened a lot of these test pieces 'Tiny Essential Victories' a few of them turned out a tad rubbish, and that was okay, they still served a purpose as practice pieces.

However, even these small steps sometimes felt overwhelming and I deliberately took a few steps back creatively and rediscovered the simple joy of pen and paper doodling, sketching out small abstract designs built around fleur de lys (a constant motif in my work and a shape I can literally draw with my eyes closed). No colour, no shading, no intended outcome, slowly building up my confidence and enthusiasm around my work until I felt more able to tackle bigger projects.

And then, I received a call from a past work colleague at ACON (the big LGBTQI health authority here in NSW Australia) asking if I would be interested in doing a 'Creativity for Wellness' seminar online via Zoom. I mean, I'd be interested, yeah, but was my creative confidence in a place where I could advise others?

While details of the session were being worked out, I set to work thinking about what I could talk about and what I could do/share/teach/advise during the seminar. I came up with the idea of offering the simplest, least demanding creative pastime I could think up and I chose to talk about some simple drawing and colouring in exercises. Start small was going to be my big message. I needed some simple black and white line drawings for the session, so I sat down in my studio and traced off the designs I had painted onto the wooden circles (pictured here). Well, once I started, I drew and I drew and I drew and I drew and I literally could not stop drawing them. They flowed out.

I never studied art. I studied fashion and a tutor at fashion college once gave me some essential advice that I doubt I would have gotten in a pretentious art school; he said 'The magic of creativity only comes when it's ready, it's like a shit, if it's not ready, it won't come out, don't try to force it because at best you'll produce a wet fart.' I didn't offer this sage advice during the 'Creativity for Wellness' session as I can never say it out loud without giggling, but I offer it here along with the theme of that session which was: let's be as kind and gentle with ourselves as we can and see what we can then create. Think about the scale of what we expect from ourselves. Even during such times as a global pandemic, do not try to look after anybody else until you have looked after yourself.

But you know, also, regardless of what's happening in the world, take time to just appreciate your own tiny essential victories as you create them.

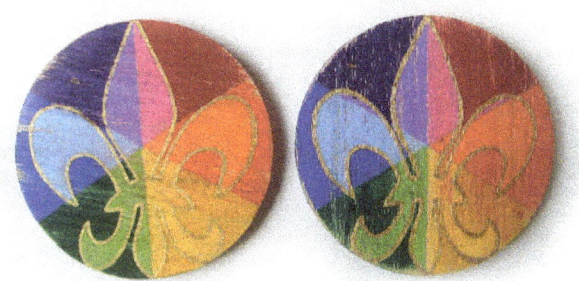

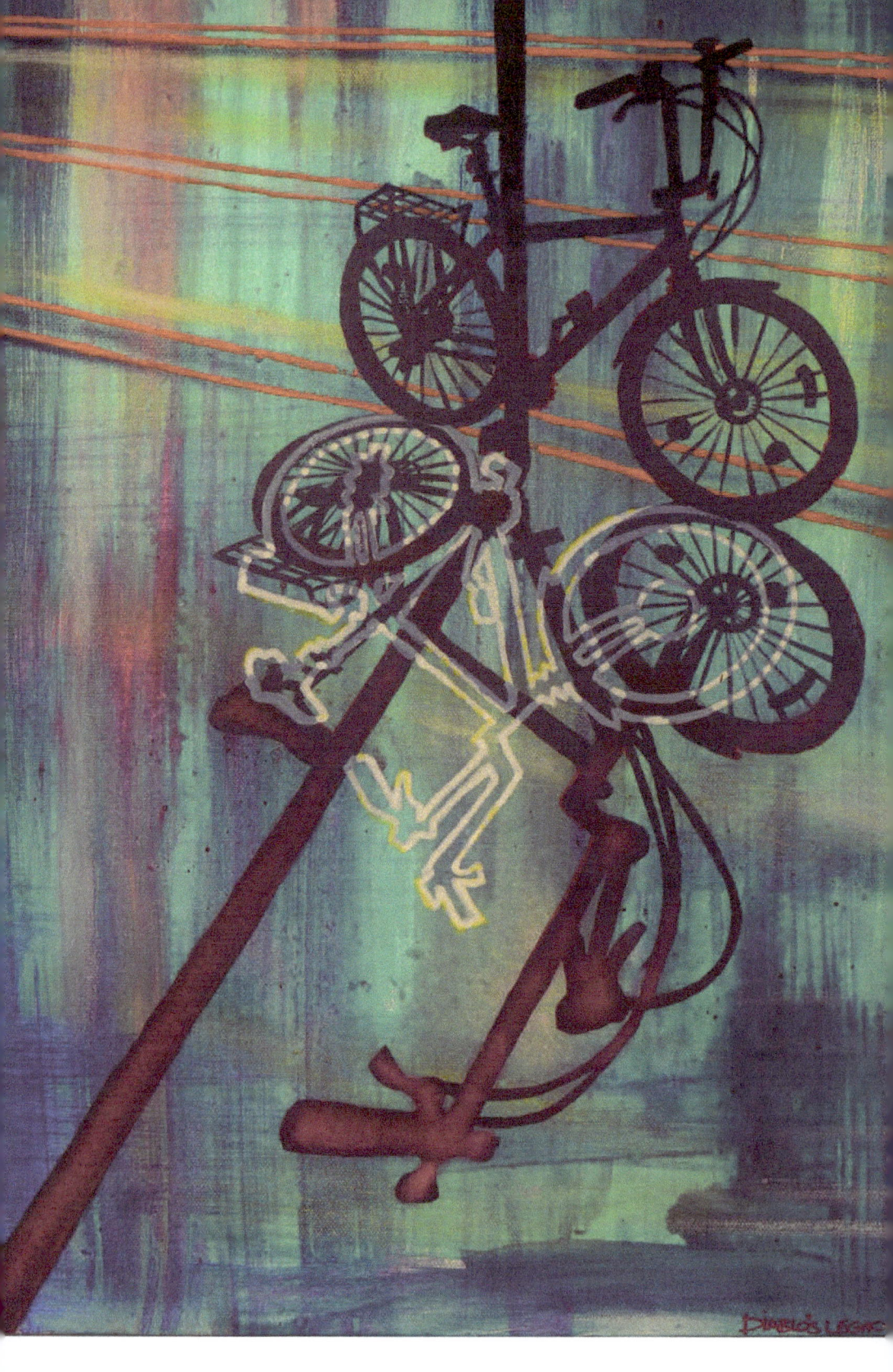
DIABLO'S LEGAS

DIABLO'S SHADOW

This chapter isn't really about my painting called 'Diablo's Shadow' but more about the person who inspired that painting, many others and actually inspires lots of different elements within my work.

While still new to Sydney, I lived in a tiny apartment high up in a block overlooking Taylor Square. It was my first time of ever really living alone and I loved it. I'd like to boast that men came and went, so to speak, and it was a saloon doored swinging bachelor pad, and I suppose it was, kind of, but mostly I was pushing off on a bit of a voyage of self-discovery, so my sex life wasn't as ridiculously rampant as it could have been.

I started dating a man who was ten years my senior called Steve, and I moved apartments within the building into Steve's even tinier studio apartment (all one room), he was a bit more sorted than I was, mostly, and although I think we both knew the relationship wasn't made to last forever, we just really enjoyed each other's company. Also, his apartment was up on the ninth floor so had better views of the harbour and you know us gays are all about water views.

Steve was a big chunky, crazily sexy bear of a man and the manager of a bar just across the road from where we lived. The bar was called Manacle and was exactly the kind of seedy gay bar you would see in movies that feature seedy gay bars. It was in the basement of a big old heritage listed building, it was dark, and there were no lights in the toilets. On weekends it was ram packed with half naked men with facial hair and hairy chests, sweat would drip off the ceiling, and it was completely fabulous. There were gigantic bowls of peanuts, still in their shells, dotted around the place and as you walked around it was almost like walking on crisp autumn leaves because of the slight romantic crunch of peanut shells underfoot. Although, if you were brave enough to delve in to grab a handful of peanuts, you'd also undoubtably collect at least one or two cockroaches as well. It was good fun watching these big beary, hairy men, standing around looking all butch and manly, suddenly emit a high pitch scream and start slapping their own arms as a surprise cockroach made a break for freedom. I decided early on never to touch the peanuts. Also, it was easily the kind of place where you didn't just have to rely on the peanuts for protein, if you get my drift…

Another ex-boyfriend of mine, a sweetie called Flynn, who was really just in the process of coming out, bless him, needed a job and I asked Steve to give him some shifts at Manacle. Talk about a baptism of fire, straight from not telling anyone he was gay to working in the gayest place in Christendom, but hey, he loved it and took to it like a slut to water.

In amongst all the other staff, along with Steve and Flynn, there was another fella that made up my dream team of gay bar mates and that was a right little cutie called Diablo.

Ever since arriving in Sydney I had noticed on the streets somebody had been chalking around the outline of bicycle shadows. There would also be cryptic messages and abstract patterns sketched out in identical simple white chalk and I often wondered about them and it turned out Diablo was the artist responsible.

He would often work in Manacle until the early hours and then wander the streets of Surry Hills and Darlinghurst with sticks of chalk in hand and spend the early hours watching the sun come up, capturing the shape of receding shadows in a thick white outline suggesting both death, history and somehow, to me, the passing of and importance of time. His chalk work was really beautiful, simple yet eye-catching and also, somehow with its lack of permanence, quite emotive and melancholic. From the very start I was a fan.

Diablo also had recently started making sculptures, using things that he had found lying around. Although this part of his art practice was still in its infancy, again his natural talent shone through. He had studied basket weaving and had a natural ability to load a quite simple subject with the same emotions as his chalk graffiti.

I was always a bit intimidated by Diablo. I just felt very dull and un-special in his presence. At that point I was dabbling with being creative. However, it was definitely a pastime and not a profession or vocation. I worked in retail and made costumes on the side, I was painting and drawing a little, but it wasn't the main part of what I was about. I think Diablo could sniff out the wannabe and lack of commitment in me. He was always the real deal. He was an artist who lived his artistry. At that point I certainly wasn't. Unfortunately, and as is often the case in the brilliantly gifted, he had his demons and let's just say, he enjoyed the pleasures that life had to offer and always loved a good party. Good on him.

Truth be told I secretly really wanted to be Diablo. I was vaguely aware of this at the time, but looking back it seems glaringly obvious, I wanted to be the popular, funny, spontaneous person also casually filled with the spectacular creative energy that he was. He was edgy, I like to think I came across as thoughtful, but he was really thoughtful, talented and loads of other far more interesting things as well. I clearly remember watching him at work in Manacle, he'd often wear a dark blue jumpsuit with most of the buttons tantalisingly (such a good word) undone on the front and he'd work his way through the crowd, collecting empty glasses but saying hi and hugging nearly everyone, and I'd think, why cant that be me? He had also studied at one of the best art schools in Australia and this tapped into my insecurities about never studying art. Diablo was a similar height to me, a similar build and just a few years younger, but we were at really different points in life. He had a very natural and likeable confidence about himself. Like a magnet, he attracted interesting and fabulous people to him naturally because of his own awesomeness. He and my ex, Flynn became really tight besties and they became known as a bit of a terribly fun twosome and were always getting into mischief and living the non-stop party life. The kind of life that always looks so much fun.

After about six months Steve and I broke up. Although we stayed good friends, he moved out of the apartment and then decided to leave Sydney for a while. In hindsight, without meaning to I think I messed Steve about a little bit and this is a very public apology for that. Manacle changed owners and became less seedy, less fun. It lasted a few years after Steve's departure in different forms but eventually closed and became a very straight R and B nightclub. I carried on living in the apartment for about a year and a half and then decided to go back to England and, since the apartment was such a (small, but) good one I asked around if anybody wanted to take over my lease.

I had stayed in touch with Diablo as he had also left Manacle, but unfortunately since he left there his demons had seemed to slightly get the better of him. I wouldn't exactly say the partying had gotten out of hand, but I do think it was beginning to take its toll. I bumped into him one day in a café and told him the apartment was going to be available and since he was looking for somewhere to live, he happily took over the lease.

He moved in as I moved out, and I remember he had this absolutely huge fish tank, which appeared to be full of nothing other than smelly green slime, although that he assured me he had fish (and possibly other creatures) cheerfully living in! The day he moved in the elevator stopped working (well, it never worked!) and it took about four people to carry the tank up the nine floors of stairs.

I ended up staying in London for just under three years, and since this was really before the internet had kicked off, I lost track of a lot of people I'd been friends with in Sydney.

When I got back to Australia my head was all over the place, but I tried to reconnect with a lot of my old Sydney friends. Now Diablo wasn't necessarily someone that I was that friendly with, so I didn't search him out initially, but fate threw us together again as we bumped into each other on the street.

He had lived in that apartment for the previous three years, pretty much up until the week before my return. He had come home to the apartment one day and found the slime filled fish tank had exploded and coated his apartment with incredibly stinky green goo. The evil stinky slime had also streamed down the walls of several floors of apartments underneath and, so not totally unsurprisingly, he had been sharply evicted.

I did have to laugh at the tale, it was typical Diablo. He had moved in with Flynn, into a cool apartment over a shop in Darlinghurst. The two of them still had a really incredible bond, and again I found myself a smidgeon envious of him. Diablo's energy had changed though. He wasn't as 'impish' and lighthearted as before I left. He had grown a big bushy beard, lost a couple of teeth and his self-care wasn't always as good as it could have been. Although still utterly adorable and charming, he seemed to carry a bit of emotional weight and I noticed him looking away from me a lot when we chatted. He was now a lot more involved in his sculpture and his work had really progressed.

He had an exhibition a few months after we reconnected, and it became clear how his work had evolved. He was making larger, bolder sculptures made from natural fibres and found items held together with coloured threads, perfectly constructed and built to form beautiful freestanding structures. I was painting now too a lot more seriously, but his work was miles ahead of mine. The gallery that he was showing in had glasses of wine on sale for 'a gold coin donation' and while chatting with Diablo on the opening night he sheepishly asked me to buy him a glass of wine as he was completely broke and didn't have a gold coin to his name.

The show was an absolute sell out and it really became clear to me how much both he and his work were loved and had found their place within Sydney's art scene and alternative queer community. Again, I found myself jealous, this time specifically of his success and popularity, and although I loved him to bits I kind of distanced myself a little from him.

Over the coming years I saw my own art practice begin to thrive. Although I'm no Diablo, I think my work has found its place within the art scene and it now connects with a good amount of people. My friendship with Diablo became a strange thing where we kind of changed places. As my confidence grew, his seemed to weaken somewhat. His health definitely took a bit of a turn for the worse and he began to suffer badly from anxiety. He and I would occasionally meet up for coffees (usually at the café under the old apartment where we had both lived) and he would try and push those catch ups into drunken benders, he preferred beer to coffee. Don't get me wrong, I certainly like a drink, but with my creative and clever friends, such as Diablo, I prefer to be fully conscious around them to hear and consider whatever they have to say. Again, these meetings just left me feeling a bit dull and unadventurous, I was still the dull one and Diablo the joyously sociable party boy. We can all only ever really be ourselves, and truth be told, I've never been a good drunk, but yeah in hindsight I could have let loose a little more.

He kept exhibiting work and as is often the case, his art sold well, which then created a demand, which became a more consuming, in fact all-consuming, part of his life. He became a popular and well-respected professional artist. His work was fabulously otherworldly and developing into a really solid artistic output. However frustratingly for those around him who cared for him, he was putting his creative output before his own wellbeing.

With my own creative process, I am aware it can envelop me and blanket me in a way that isn't a good thing. I lean constantly on my self-built handrails (made of string, glue, bottle caps, considerate relationships and self-care) to stop me from falling into the abys. I know when to step away or at least step to the side a little in order to not completely drain myself. I don't think Diablo had that understanding as a resource. He had people around him who loved him, but I don't think he was acting on their advice. He and I had a lot of respect for each other as artists, but I began to feel he was mocking me slightly (and never with malice) for being so well-behaved and clean living. I don't really think I am, but I guess these things are always on a sliding scale. He was a very good person to chat with about my evolving art practice. He 'got it' about the frustrations of being a queer artist in a straight art world and he, like me only was prepared to play in the art world's corrupt boardgame if it was by our own rules.

My partner, Ryan and I bought various pieces from him including a series of four sketches of his from an exhibition he had, that were quite disturbing, bleak and unapologetic self-portraits, but I loved them because I hardly ever saw his drawings. They were quite dark and macabre pen on paper sketches and when I came to pick them up he had a shoe box filled with other sketches he said were part of the same series and he wanted me and Ryan to have them. Another time he bought a painting of mine, a still life of beer bottles and chip packets, which made me giggle that he had connected with that particular piece so much. At this point we'd been friends for almost 20 years, and I was really used to just having him around. I'd often bump into him in the local streets, at coffee shops or even see him sitting outside a bar (sometimes even having what we'd affectionately call a 'breakfast beer') he seemed such a constant, although, increasingly, a distant connection to everything I knew about Sydney. Yup, I suppose I just took him for granted.

It became really clear to me that Diablo was one of those artists that just didn't really recognise or appreciate his own amazing potential and talent. His self-care, which to me is very connected to self-worth, and his overall health were slowly deteriorating. We talked about that, but it wasn't something to he was comfortable to chat about, so it would be awkwardly joked about but brushed off. It was sad to watch, but nothing I could reach in to adjust. He and Flynn were still party boys and as we all were getting older, there was an overall feeling that I was settling down, growing duller and more boring, while they were still edgy and cool, and how could I argue with that?

One day I walked out of my place of work and found him sitting hunched up on a park bench in the street watching passers-by. Initially he said he had been waiting for me, but it became clear he didn't really know quite what he was doing, and he was really agitated and nervy. We chatted a while and it was actually a good chat where I told him how much I valued him and how I wanted him to sort himself out and I walked him round to the local doctor at Taylor Square and insisted he go in. I remember he looked me right in the eye and said I was a good friend. I messaged him later to check up, but didn't hear anything back from him for a while, however weeks later I saw him again and he told me he had walked into the doctors, done a 180 once I'd left him, and walked out straight to the nearest pub. He was an adult, and that was his decision.

It absolutely broke my heart, but came as little surprise, when I got a message from a friend telling me of Diablos death a couple of years ago. It's such a cliché to talk about 'the star that burns twice as bright burns for half as long' but this was never truer than in Diablo's case. His light was magnificent and illuminated so many around him. One of his many health issues had caught up with him and taken him in the early hours one morning as he was halfway through working on a sculpture. He had been living with a long-time partner, had been happy and, as far as I know, died while doing what he loved most; living a creative life. As I think it through now, I think he probably would have been okay with how everything played out, and I guess when your time's up who wouldn't want to go quickly and happily.

He was only a couple of years younger than me, and I'm fine with saying it out loud, a lot more naturally talented. It was such a shame to see him go so soon, I don't doubt he had a lot of creativity left in him. He was always, from the very first moment I met him, a genuinely brilliant creative; it was in his blood. But in a way, it was that which sealed his fate. I never saw him apply brakes on to anything: his life, his love of life and his art practise, everything in his life was there for the taking.

Anyone who is familiar with my paintings knows I paint bikes a lot. They are an obsession of mine and I completely accredit my initial involvement with them to Diablo, if it wasn't for his bright white chalk marks around bike shadows to draw me into the concept of bikes as a metaphor then maybe I would never have gotten to this point.

Along with a few other sculptural pieces, I still have the four sketches I bought from him up on my walls at home. I see his face every day, and therefore every day I see within those pictures the darkness that ultimately consumed him. They remind me to always hold on to my handrails whist tiptoeing around the creative abyss (or oversized inverted arsehole, whichever you want to call it) in my head. They are a constant reminder of him, but also to me of what he could have achieved, and I like to think a little of Diablos shadow's and outlines still reach out and influence my work. I often encourage it to and if, by any chance, from the other side (whatever that means) he can lend me some of his coolness and edge, I'll happily take it. I don't think I will ever not be reminded of him, whenever I see bike shadows, white chalk lines, blue boiler suits or hypermasculine men slapping themselves and screaming at cockroaches.

These foolish things remind me of you. I miss our chats buddy.

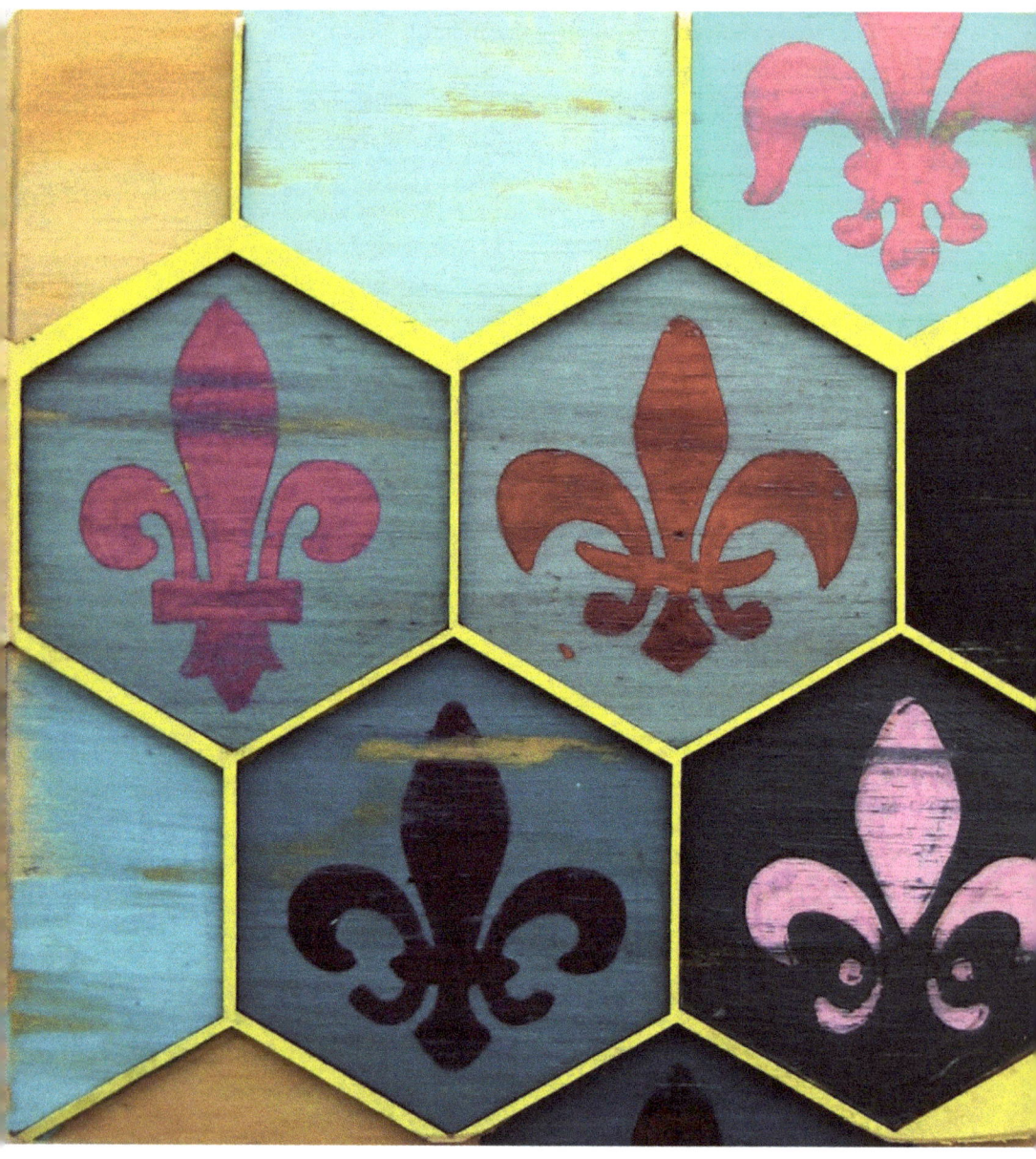

HONEYCOMB WISHES

I like this piece.

It is small, it is strange, to me it is perfectly formed, and it invokes a sense of (very) scaled down spectacle. That is what I intended it to do and I was very pleased when I finished it and it perfectly met my intentions in those regards. There are few moments more satisfying than standing back from something you created and feeling calm and achieved. Lovely.

Howfuckingever ... it just got rejected from an art prize.

You know that thing that your elder sibling used to do to you when you were bored kids, where they would lift your hand and repetitively use it to slap you in the face. It was normally accompanied with a chorus of 'why are you hitting yourself, why are you hitting yourself!'

Well sometimes creating art, and putting it out into the world, feels a lot like that. Not everyone is a fan and not even 'fans' (what does that even mean?) will like every piece. Sometimes the most absolutely crushing harsh and vicious thing you can say to an artist is, 'Can you explain it ...?'

OhIfuckingtellya ...

And don't even get me STARTED on how, in Australia, so much of the 'Art World' (what does that even mean?) is built around winning painting prizes!! I enter them lots because you've just gotta 'be in it to win it'. And although I hate myself for it, yes, on some level I obviously crave acceptance. But you know what entering and being constantly rejected from art competitions feels like?

Lemmefuckingtellya ...

You know when your dickhead friend learns to drive and they say they'll give you a lift somewhere and they come to pick you up and you go to open the car door and they pull forward a little bit? Just a little nudge forward, but enough so you feel like a fool. And you can see them inside the car thinking they are fucking hysterically funny, when obviously they really aren't? Well, it's not exactly that, but it is, when they do that pulling forward a bit thing twelve times in a fucking row, and you hate yourself because you know they can't be trusted. But you have no other choice than to try to open that car door yet again because you really need to get where you're going, so you go for the handle AGAIN and they pull forward AGAIN. Well, yeah, that's it, that's the feeling.

Honesttofuckinggod …

And you know what's worse, when someone I know *does* get into an art prize that I entered but didn't get in and they will not stop talking about it on social media. That's so fucking annoying, that is noisy eater level annoying. I really don't need to hear this. Fucking shudup! I know, I get it, how delicious for you. Yum yum! But please close your mouth or at least eat quickly, some of us are really quite famished over here!!

BloodyannoyingFuckingfuckingfuckingfuckfuck …

Anyway, Honeycomb wishes I love you even if no one else does.

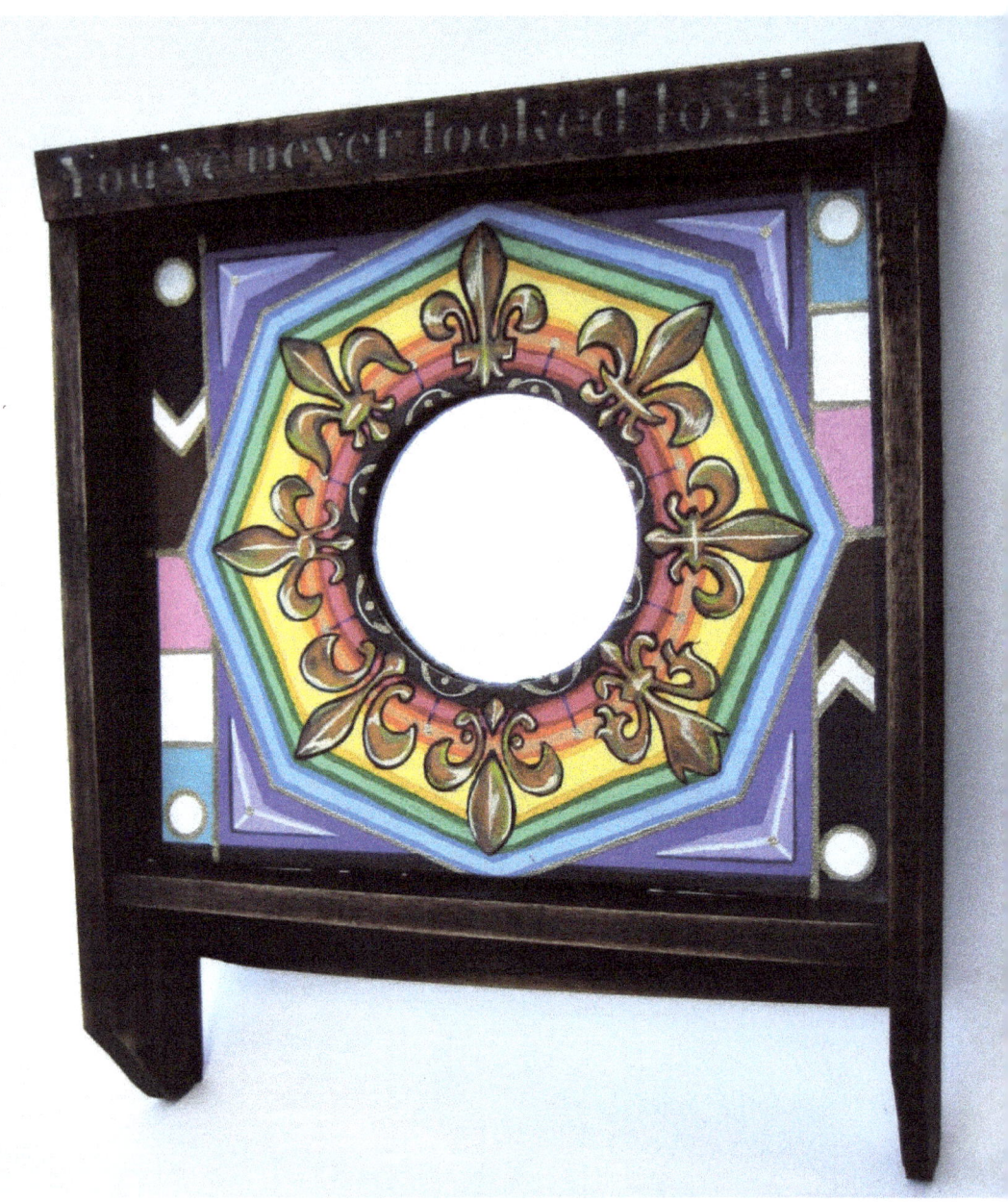

YOU'VE NEVER LOOKED LOVELIER

This is a piece about vanity, but also about how vanity, within reason, is not necessarily a bad thing.

It's not very obvious from the photo here, but the piece has a mirror in the middle, and it says the words 'You've never looked lovelier' across the top.

The colours used within the painting element are from the Black Lives Matter and Trans Pride flags, basically what I wanted to say with this piece is, we are all made up from what we have around us; or, you may be something, but none of us are really anything without our communities around us (holding us up and appreciating us).

I like the 'Mirror, mirror, on the wall' aspect of this piece. A mirror that always tells you that you have never looked lovelier. And I mean who's to say it's wrong, at some point, there must be an exact point that you will look your absolute best, but who's really to say when that is? Surely our beauty and attractiveness is all relative and subjective. I don't exclusively believe that youth equals beauty, some of us grow into our looks and get better with age. The message to the piece, which is written across the top is meant as a message of empowerment, an offer of support, if that is needed.

I can be a vain man. I am the first to admit it. But I think vanity and self-exploration are an important part of my creative output: the interest and objectification of self and beauty, in all their unorthodox aspects is a healthy thing to explore. If we can use these things in a positive way then that's a good thing, right? Obviously as with most things there's a line, vanity = good, narcissism = bad!

I remember years ago walking around an exhibition at a large gallery and as well as taking in the show I couldn't help but notice a rather attractive gentleman wandering around while I was. He and I checked each other out as we both walked in and out of the exhibition rooms. Gays tend to do that, it's who we are. Towards the end of the exhibition, he and I found ourselves both standing in front of a large painting and he leant in towards me and softly whispered, 'You are the most beautiful thing in here.' And as I stood there giggling and blushing like a giddy schoolgirl, he walked away, never to be seen again.

Well, now, I don't mind telling you, had this happened at an earlier point in my life and I'd been single at the time I would have fucked him till his head dropped off, however, it was really just the easygoing, casual interaction that was so wonderful. I was in a relationship at the time, but that wasn't the issue as such, I usually negotiate an openness in relationships, I just didn't feel a need to take that interaction anywhere further. It was such a sweet, innocent, yet hot as all hell, thing to happen.

At the time I had a good friend called Robert (still a good friend, but he selfishly moved to Queensland so I hardly ever see him) and we met up that evening for noodles and wine. Robert is a very honest friend and I trust his judgement perfectly. I happily recounted the interaction I had during that day at the gallery as Robert just rolled his eyes.

'Were you wearing your scarf pulled up and your hat pulled down at the time?' he asked me.

I nodded sadly and sucked on my noodles, I had been, and I understood completely what he was getting at.

Now my point to this story is that, just like most of us, I enjoy being found attractive. However, I don't take that side of myself too seriously at all. I know in the right light, right outfit and with the right make-up, I can look okay. Yay for me. But I have never taken my appearance as a definite resource. It's not a thing I've ever relied on or a resource I've purposely exploited.

I have a friend who is an artist here in Sydney and his following is made up, pretty much, entirely of gay men and his work often features his own nudity and sexual availability. On social media he posts self-sketched nudes a lot. I can safely say I've seen his penis a lot more than I'd ever want to. It's not a bad penis, but he definitely treads the line between art and unsolicited dick pics. Good on him though, he has a creative output and he is putting it all out there (literally) he knows his audience and he very probably makes more money out of his art practice than I do, and, yeah, but nah. Creative vanity = good, sexy narcissism = bad. However, that's just my opinion in regard to my artist friend's work and is in no way a definitive thought process about nudity or sexuality in art. That's a whole nuther conversation.

I had an idea about a different piece similar to 'You've never looked lovelier' a while ago, but the idea just didn't solidify in my mind. There was a vital part missing, however a while ago I was taking my dog (oh Lil Matey Dog, how I loves ya) for a walk and he stopped to do a pee on the side of a skip, as you do, and glancing in the skip I saw an assortment of old drawers. They were quite battered and old, and I got to thinking about how these essential things were only valued at certain points in certain situations and settings.

Pop! That's like me I thought! Lightbulb moment! Something that is essential and appreciated only in certain lights and certain situations.

It was the missing piece of the puzzle and into the skip I went, with Matey looking at me like I was a being possessed! I purposely selected the oldest most knackered drawer (and one of the few not filled with rainwater). I stretched the canvas, cut a hole in the middle of it, placed a mirror behind it and painted the piece framed inside the drawer. It's not a massive piece so the painting was quite an 'intimate' (for want of a better word) thing to do and while I was painting the piece, I had to stare at my own reflection a lot.

It's a good job I'm okay with my face, otherwise that would have added to the challenge. Luckily I didn't feel the need to pull up my scarf and pull down my hat …

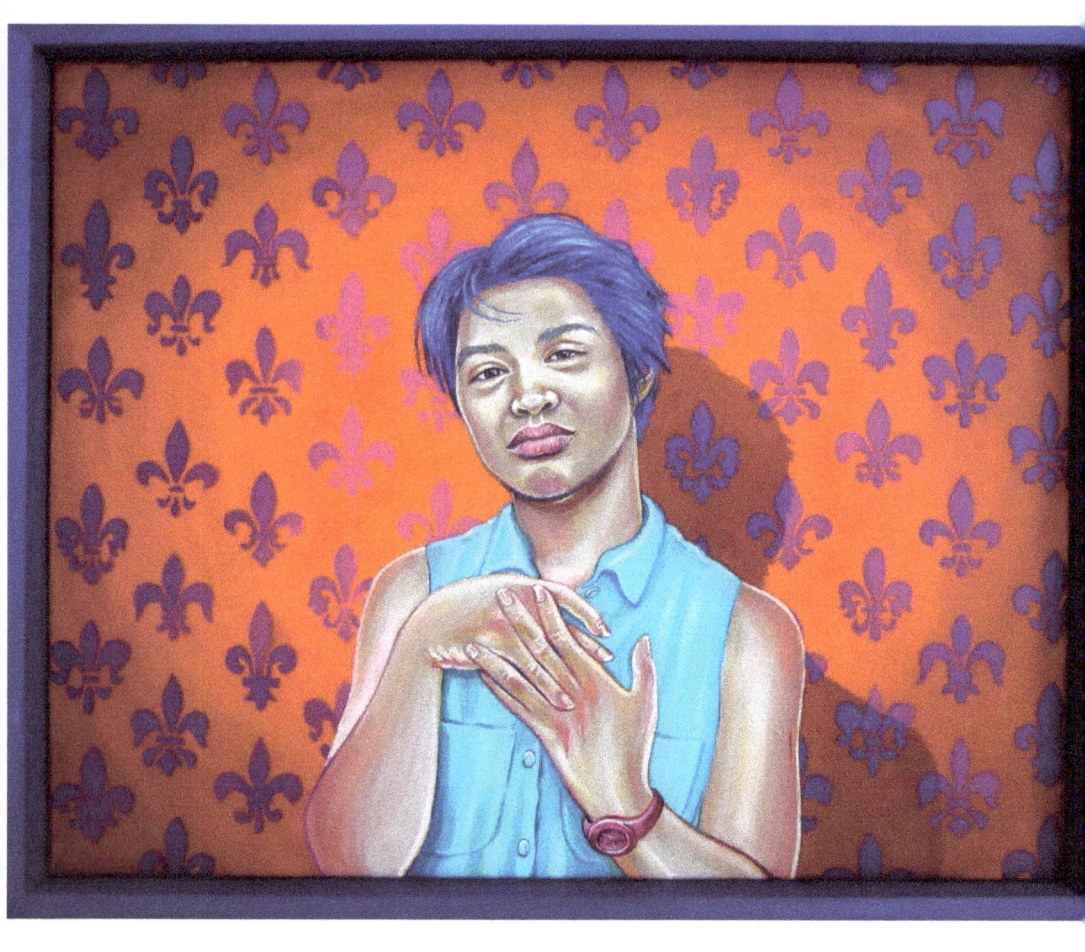

MIREN

Now without wanting to 'big up myself' as I believe youngsters say nowa days. I am superhuman. Yup, I have superpowers. However, my superpowers aren't some pointless silly things like being able to pick up a car, x-ray vision, or fly straight up in the air, phfft, USELESS!! My superpowers are far more exciting and practical for the modern world. Take a seat, puny human, I shall list them for you forthwith.

1. CONFIDENCE

You know the expression 'strut with the confidence of a very average white man' well, lemmefuckingtellya, that's written about me!! I am that average white man. My manifestation of my superpower of confidence gives me the joyous and unending ability to not have to put up with other people's nonsense! With a swish of my fabulous, yet quite stylishly understated cape, I am often even confident enough just walk away mid-bullshit. True story. I know, it's super, I just don't care! Small note however, I didn't have this superpower until recently, it developed gradually over time, kind of in correlation with my occasional mini superpower of not really giving a fuck what people think of me. There are, unfortunately, still those in the word who will try to wield kryptonite against me, namely arrogance and privilege, and sometimes I buckle when these are used against me. Damn you my evil foes. But fuck it, I'm getting stronger over time and I hope one day these things will be useless against me. AND I WILL BECOME INVINCIBLE.

2. INVISIBILITY

To many people, I have found I can become quite, quite transparent. To straight people, mostly men, as an obviously queer person, they often look right through me! I'M JUST NOT THERE AT ALL! It is fabulous. Although this superpower is a bit of a double-edged sword and it can become frustrating in certain situations, let's say, at the bar in a straight pub trying to buy drinks, or in a business situation of mainly straight men, when the cloak of invisibility is draped over me without my consent, but I refer you, dear reader to superpower number 1. Try to dissolve me into the background at your peril fellas, the more you ignore me the louder and more vivid I become! Just remember, if you didn't see me coming, it's because you chose to look right through me! If the way I look makes you look away to make me disappear from view then fine, you miss out. I can walk in heels bigger than your dick, now that's a REAL superpower!

3. TALKING TO WOMEN

I have the ability to talk to women! Now, firstly this should not be a superpower at all, but sadly after chatting to most of my female friends it appears it is. This also might seem very everyday and humdrum as a lot of people have this (clearly most other women, for example), but very few men really do. I get the oppression. I've endured the gaslighting. I understand the 'stay in your lane' stares as I step forward to make my point. I experienced firsthand the 'I'll give you time to talk but I won't take you seriously' face that a lot of women are very familiar with from men. Oh yes sister, I fucking get it. Now, admittedly my experience in this evil dark realm has been as a part-time casual and I get that I can remove my super hero mask at will and pass in the everyday world of men should I choose, however, my limited exposure to this alternative reality, is still more than a lot of men (even 'straight-acting' gay men) have had, and it has made me both super aware and super vigilant. In my day job I work as a part time in an art supplies store and my only other co-worker (it's a small shop) is a woman of colour. EVERY FUCKING DAY I work there I see an example of sexism, racism or micro aggressions within those prejudices. EVERY FUCKING DAY. Without ever requesting it people also certainly try to burden her with their unwanted gift of invisibility. I'm a portrait painter, I have super observational skills, my eyes are practically fucking bionic in this respect. My eyes pick up the tiniest of details. While it exhausts me as a bystander, I realise it must utterly, utterly fucking exhausting my co-worker (pictured in the painting above), and she has to engage her own super abilities to become super fucking patient and super resilient to not let that bullshit fuck her over. And she never gets to change out of her mask and cape. As an older white male, people occasionally approach me as 'the manager', however she and I work together as a dastardly duo to expose and educate. My favourite thing in such a situation is to fix people with the blankest of blank stares and ask, 'Why did you just presume I was the manager?'

4. FARTING AT WILL

I possess the ability to fart at will! Basically, as a vegan, and please excuse the directness here, I always have one loaded in the barrel, so to speak. Stealth is my secret weapon (although so is an almost malicious eagerness). I am the dark lord of the silent but deadly. Please refer to the situations listed above. Mess with me or my kind and I'll mess with your nostrils and before you know what's going to hit you I'll fix you with a 'Urgh, what have you done' stare so that, milli-seconds before the attack coming your way, I've already accused you of it, and no one does indignant offence like the middle-aged British male. Annoy me and I will drop one, I will accuse you, I will walk away, and your plan for world dominance will be destroyed. Not all heroes wear capes, some wear lose legged shorts.

5. HUMOUR

I was born in the North East of England in a working-class family. There was nothing that could not be turned into a joke and laughed at. Nothing. It gets me through every shitty oppressive bullshit rejection prejudice situation I have ever encountered, and it makes every weapon at your disposal pointless. My weakness is that it might take a while, but eventually, I will be able to laugh off your attack, your disregard or your rejection. Come at me with the absolute worst you have; but realise your worst is just you waving a dildo at a knife fight; you have nothing. I have the wicked, dark and piss-funny humour of my people to protect me. Please note, my costume for this is less of a super-hero style sexy body armour but more like a giant hot dog costume and a cap with straws for drinking beer, but it works all the same.

6. A PLATFORM

I have a platform! Not much of a one, I will give you that, but people seem vaguely interested in what I'm doing sometimes, and that's enough. This, with a combination of my powers listed above (okay, possibly without the farting) means I have a metaphorical microphone or a stage that many may not. I promise I will always try my best to use my powers for good, but I warn you, I'm not above being petty or childish, again please refer to superpower number 1: I care little of what you think.

7. STILL LEARNING

I am certainly not ashamed to say I'm still learning! And you know what, sadly not everyone has this skill. I mean, for fucks sake, it's not hard. As the superhero of superheroes, Maya Angelou, once said, 'Do the best you can until you know better. Then when you know better, do better.'

If you are too scared to admit that you, like us all, are still learning from life as you go, it's best you don't leave your house. It's a big scary world out there for those that want to stay hopelessly yet happily ignorant.

8. I'M LIKEABLE

People seem to like me! And you know what that means... I get to recruit! I get to assemble a team of likeminded superheroes who are just as damaged by the world as I am, and we get to plot to take over the world with our damaged, humorous, super resilience. Bwahahaha! I love acting as a mentor for younger artists, people who I know are not going to be offered best chances by the world, for whatever reason. I connect best with the disadvantaged and the 'other-ised' by society and I happily bring them in to my crime-fighting-collective and empower them with all the fucked-up lessons I've learnt. You see, really, I don't want to use my powers to take over the world, I just want to make the world a better place, certainly for those that may not have fully realised their own potential creative superpowers like I've been given the chance to. Being able to enable and empower others is a very special power to have and I never abuse it. Together we are all stronger, I get to build and shape community and that is something I'm very pleased and proud of. Picture the scene, as in all superhero films, in slow motion, me and my sexy rag-tag group all move to the camera towards you, capes billowing and talents and gifts at the ready. Maybe just pity the one standing immediately to my left pulling a face as I high kick, because, well, you know, whoops, I can't always control all my powers at once!

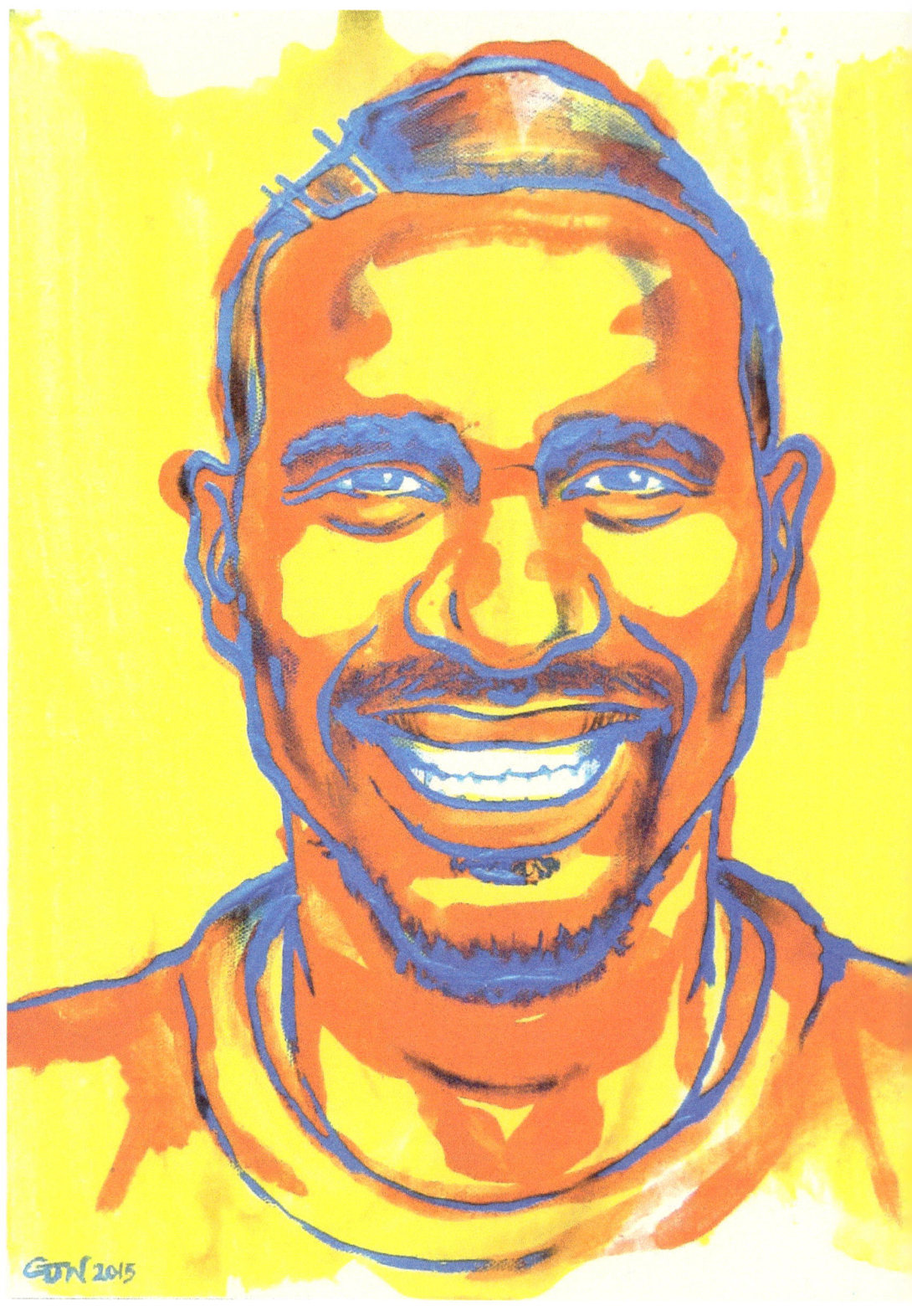

HAPPINESS

I keep intending for my 'next' work to be one of capturing happiness, and I know what you're thinking, your thinking he's going to use that old line about 'you can't say happiness without saying 'a penis', and you're quite right, I just did! Whay-hay!

However, the thought of a single painting made up of pure happiness is too hard, too out of my range of abilities at this moment in time.

I am generally a happy person. I've managed to persuade and offend my demons enough so that they give me space to operate effectively enough in the world to regularly encounter joy. I utterly value happiness as the fragile and easily losable thing that it is.

If I were a better painter, some of the scenes of happiness in my life I'd try to portray are these.

As a small child, I used to love it when my mum and dad would go for drinks at a neighbours house and my mum would come back late at night smelling of perfume, drink and cigarettes and sneak in my room to 'tuck me in'. Which basically meant lying on my bed covers squishing me in and telling me how much she loved me. I remember lying there in the darkness, utterly trapped but blissfully in want of nothing more. Years later, the roles were reversed, weeks before she died and although my declarations of love were just as heartfelt, they were muddled with remorse and awkwardness. There is certainly nothing purer than a mother's love of an infant child. As an adult, I've been on the set of glamorous fashion shoots where the smell of make-up and hairspray sends me into an internal melancholic spiral.

Another moment of true happiness was dancing at a rave in a converted church in Edinburgh at some point in the 90s. Yes, this would have been a chemically enhanced high, but it was still a very real moment of bliss. I remember looking up at the huge stained-glass window and with my friends around me experiencing that very same simple happiness of my mother's cuddles and the feeling of wanting nothing more.

In the late 90s waking up next to my lover in Sydney, who happened to be a very large solidly built Pacific Islander (who could literally pick me up in one hand) and feeling so safe and warm in his arms and knowing, as he was a professional chef, I was in for a superb breakfast to come, well, once other things were out of the way first.

Cycling around London in my early twenties.

Lying on a hot rooftop terrace in Southern Spain, drinking ice cold beers, with my very best friends and laughing at our attempts at modelling ridiculously high stiletto's we'd 'borrowed' from a friend's fashion show in London the day before.

Visiting Northumberland from Sydney and taking Ryan, my partner, back to meet my family and him being welcomed with open arms, but mostly one particular afternoon of a family get together, giggling with my sisters in the kitchen while we ate sugary cakes I would never normally eat. Happiness and fun.

Hysterically laughing whilst being horribly seasick on tiny wooden 'ferries' travelling between Greek islands with best friends Beverly and Gary as I turned twenty. The world, if we lived to make it off the boat, was absolutely ours for the taking at that point.

More recently, sitting outside a rental property in Port Stephens watching birds in the morning sunlight, listening to Ryan bustling about in the kitchen and feeding Matey-dog granola out of my hand.

Although, reading back I've mentioned a fair few places I've encountered happiness on my travels, I actually do believe happiness comes from within and only happens when we relax and allow ourselves contentment with our lot, without wishing for anything more. I think I'm mostly there, most of the time, but happiness is fleeting and ebbs and flows at its own will. Obviously for every sublime sun-dappled moment listed above there is an opposing shadow-filled recollection of frustration and horror. I shan't list those here. Many artists choose to manifest and portray their demons in their work, but I prefer to make paintings that make people smile, forget their demons, disregard their worries and forgive their own shortcomings.

Life is too short and so am I.

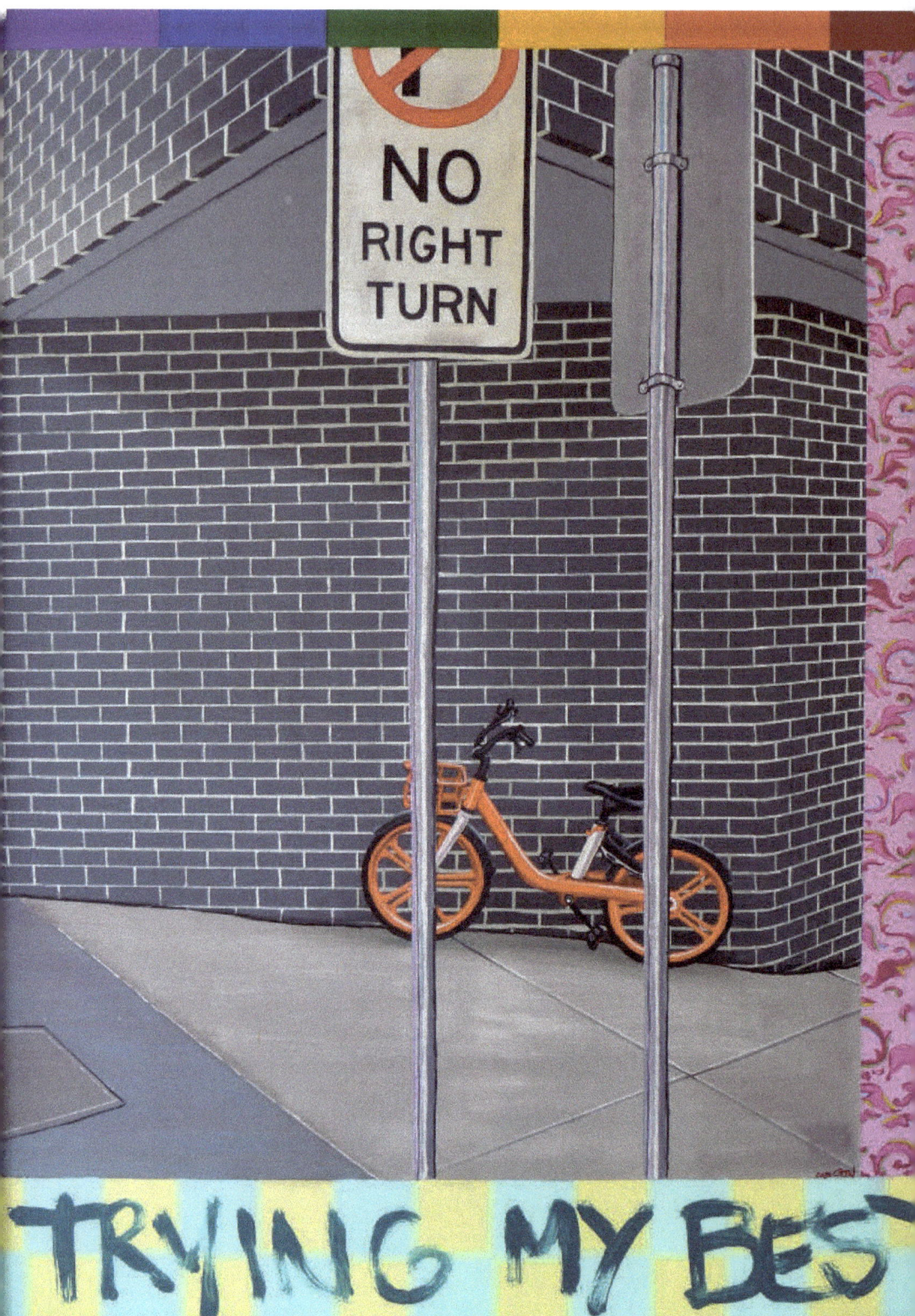

I'M TRYING MY BEST

I'm not fond of this painting.

It took me days to paint in all the brickwork. It's less of a painting and more of a punishment. It was initially meant to be a piece about Black Lives Matter. Let's say emotions were running high when I painted it, globally and personally, everything was overwhelming me, and it's now really about a few things. I can appreciate what I was trying to do, but I can't completely appreciate the outcome.

The poles in the painting represents the bars of a prison cell and it is meant to reference the corrupt incarceration rates in the US and also here in Australia of First Nations people and people of colour. I was working on the painting one particularly dark day mood wise, and I just had such an overwhelming sense of frustration and failure that I reached out, grabbed a paintbrush and wrote the words on the bottom of the painting 'I'm trying my best'.

I have always struggled with a feeling of not being good enough. It's ongoing, it's my default when things don't go right.

This manifests now as trying too hard all the time. I rarely fully relax and I always over-aim for achievements. I can't have one book out about my work; it has to be a complex three-part triptych of social commentary combined with memoir. For fucks sake, I absolutely exhaust myself, I really do.

I find paintings work best when I manage to find that sweet spot between authenticity, confidence and intention. Sometimes I know what I want to do, how to do it, what it looks like and know how to get there. It's difficult because often I know what I want to say, but my voice doesn't sound like it's my own authentic voice and what comes out can be muddled, open for mis-interpretation and badly executed.

I very rarely just paint straight onto a canvas, I overthink pretty much everything and most things are planned and graphed out. I did the writing on the bottom of the painting and then just wanted to slap myself. What had I done! It's a good job acrylic paint dries so quickly and I didn't have a chance to wipe it off.

The sign that says 'No right turn' well, obviously that symbolises my political leanings. The masses of brickwork became too labored and it doesn't read well, the pink fleur down the side, well that didn't work out exactly as I wanted it to either.

Basically, some things just don't fucking go as planned. Years ago, when I was in therapy, I discussed how as a child I felt there were two Me's. One, the outward well-behaved child who put up with everything, did what was required and tried as hard as they could to meet people's expectations. And then there was this second, secret and disappointing me that covertly felt disconnected to everyone around them, understood failure way too well and was worried by everything and feared this, and other, truths coming out. Unfortunately, the second me was the realer one, but I spent so much time pretending to be, as much as I was able, the first one that I kind of lost myself. Children are always authentic when left to their own devices, but I wasn't left to my own devices at all. I learnt to hide my real feelings really well and not ever allow this second, more honest me, too close to the surface.

So now as an adult, especially as a creative adult I keep searching, trying to rediscover and recover this secret authenticity and the intentions I could feel back then but would try to suppress. What is it I'm really trying to say? Some days I can almost tap into it and it seems real and available. And then some days it isn't.

A big part of my painting practice is learning to be okay with paintings, or parts of paintings I don't feel are that good. Writing, painting and all the other things I do can be really intense and I'm in the process of teaching myself it's okay to fail, be average or just not able to do something to a point where I'm happy with it.

I guess there are good days and bad days, good paintings and bad paintings, chapters that are entertaining and chapters that are too introspective and dull and all I can do is keep trying to keep things authentic and keep trying my best.

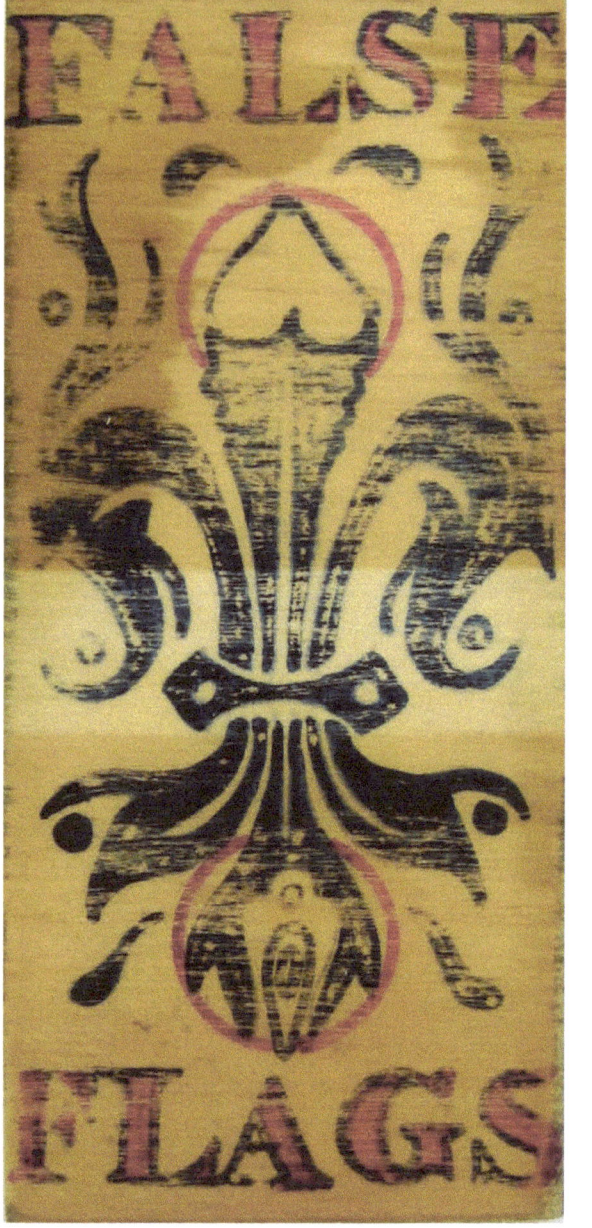

FALSE FLAGS

This piece is about how genitals are not gender.

The other day I got called a matriarch and I have to say it's one of the biggest and best compliments I have ever been paid. Gender stereotypes aren't usually something that tickle my pickle or get me off, but the idea of possibly wielding feminine energy to the good of the social structure around me is something that makes me very happy and proud.

I've had mixed results with the trying on of masculinity. I don't mind elements of it as an occasional accessory, but I struggle to find a complete outfit that I'm utterly comfortable in.

Years ago, in my early twenties, I was lucky enough to enjoy an impromptu few days in Amsterdam, with my then partner Stefan, and we decided to throw both caution and our knickers to the wind and go to a sexysexy men-only club, even though we knew it was going to be mostly leather, fetish and uniform and that wasn't really our thing. Back then in my dumb-dizzy-disco days, I thought we should give it a go, I mean, what could possibly go wrong, right?

Since Stefan and I weren't really into men-only sex clubs, we didn't have any fetish clothing to wear, so we both just wore all black (caps, singlets and jeans) and that managed to be enough to just get us in the club, although we stuck out quite obviously as tourists.

We went to a very typical Amsterdam café on the way and had a suggestively bitter chocolate brownie and, without thinking through outcomes thoroughly, we unwisely also shared a delightful jazz cigarette. Unsurprisingly, I don't mind telling you, by the time we got to the club we were a tad giggly and quite lightheaded.

We pooled our somewhat limited cash to buy a couple of beers and wandered around for a while, but we realised, quite early on, this place just wasn't for us. We'd been told, however, somewhere here was a particular room where men went to cruise each other, and it was there that most of the 'action' went on and we wanted to at least see something penis-like or shaped before heading back to our basic budget hotel.

After much vague wandering around and giggling at ourselves, we found a discreet staircase that led us down to a long slim, barely lit room. A fair smattering of men lined the sides of this room, leaning against the walls, drinking from beer bottles and cruising each other. There were barely any lights in this room, save for an exit sign above the doorway to the staircase that we'd just walked down. A matching doorway and light stood at the other end of the room, but other than that, there weren't a lot of additional design features.

A quick digression. I had on a different occasion been in what is often called a 'backroom' before in London. But in that instance, unfortunately, the man I had decided to have sex with owned several cats and since I'm am very allergic, I had a massive, continual sneezing fit, and got collectively asked to leave by the other users of the dark and silent backroom, because I was apparently spoiling the mood for everyone. Meanwhile, back in Amsterdam …

The dull thud of dance music echoed from the club above, and other than that, the room was almost silent. Men posed, postured, sucked in cheeks, tried their best to look butch and angled themselves with their best side forward. Masculinity at its most performed and contrived, but also, I'll admit, not without its charm. Stefan and I found a small gap and joined the men in standing around and nonchalantly staring each other out. We both avoided each other's gaze as we knew we'd set each other off. Normally in such situations there comes a tipping point when the sexual tension bubbles over and the men in the room start making a move on each other and body parts start getting touched, sucked, rimmed and penetrated, but we didn't seem to be anywhere near that point yet.

However, rather typically this was the moment I realised I needed to use the toilet and I whisperingly asked Stefan if he'd seen a bathroom on our earlier meander around the club. We decided that the bathroom must be up the opposite stairway that we walked in, and although feeling massively self-conscious/paranoid (from both the chocolate brownie and the situation) I broke cover and walked out into the middle of the room towards the exit doorway and dim light. It struck me at this point I was a little worse for wear and my legs didn't want to work properly. I couldn't quite seem to get the correct balance of catwalk-strut and casual-wandering! As I headed towards the slightly illuminated door, I became aware I was the focus of attention for the whole room. I pulled down my baseball cap and tried to act as inconspicuously as possible.

As I walked towards the door I realised a man was walking towards me, probably I guessed, from walking down the stairs directly in front of me. I presumed he would just walk to one side and I carried on walking straight ahead. As he walked towards me, I felt yet more paranoia and I just tried my best to focus on the ground in front of me to keep myself walking in a straight line. I could still see the man's shoes walking towards me, and I prepared myself to step aside around him as I walked. At exactly the same point I realised the man's shoes were my shoes, I walked smack into a mirror.

There was only ever one entrance and exit into this room and a large floor to ceiling mirror covered the opposite wall from where we had walked in. As I stood there, with my cap's peak flat against my face and the slow rise of shame washing over me, I had a brief moment to contemplate the situation, and you know, although the humour was not lost on me, the ridiculousness of the whole situation was the stronger realisation.

I turned to see pretty much the whole of the room giggling and laughing in various degrees at my expense, which, I'll be honest, didn't really upset me. I too started having a giggling fit. It's worth pointing out though, in amongst all of the pointing at me, all pretence at hyper-masculinity had been forgotten by this group of men.

This whole thing happened nearly thirty years ago and I can't exactly remember what happened next, but I know if this had happened today, I would have turned to the room and bowed or rather, in this instance, curtseyed! Maybe I had the confidence and self-awareness to do this at the time, maybe I didn't, I can't remember, although I like to think I did.

I know Stefan and I would have definitely fallen laughing from the club out into the street. The hyper-masculine, men-only scene has never been my kind of scene for many reasons; it's always struck me as a tad contrived. Although I'm happy it exists, it just isn't for me. In a not unrelated point, it always makes me roll my eyes when on a men-only dating app a user will list themselves as 'straight acting'. Thankfully this is happening less and less, but it's definitely still a thing. Don't 'act' at anything honey, just be yourself. That's exactly what we've all been campaigning for all of these years!

Anyway, hyper-masculinity, like hyper-religious beliefs and heightened belief in some political views just becomes problematic and toxic after a point. The enforcing of something made up never ends well. I like my men in touch with their feminine side, no matter what size, amount, shape or essence that comes in. I love a handlebar moustaches and aviator sunglasses, but only when combined with a gingham dress.

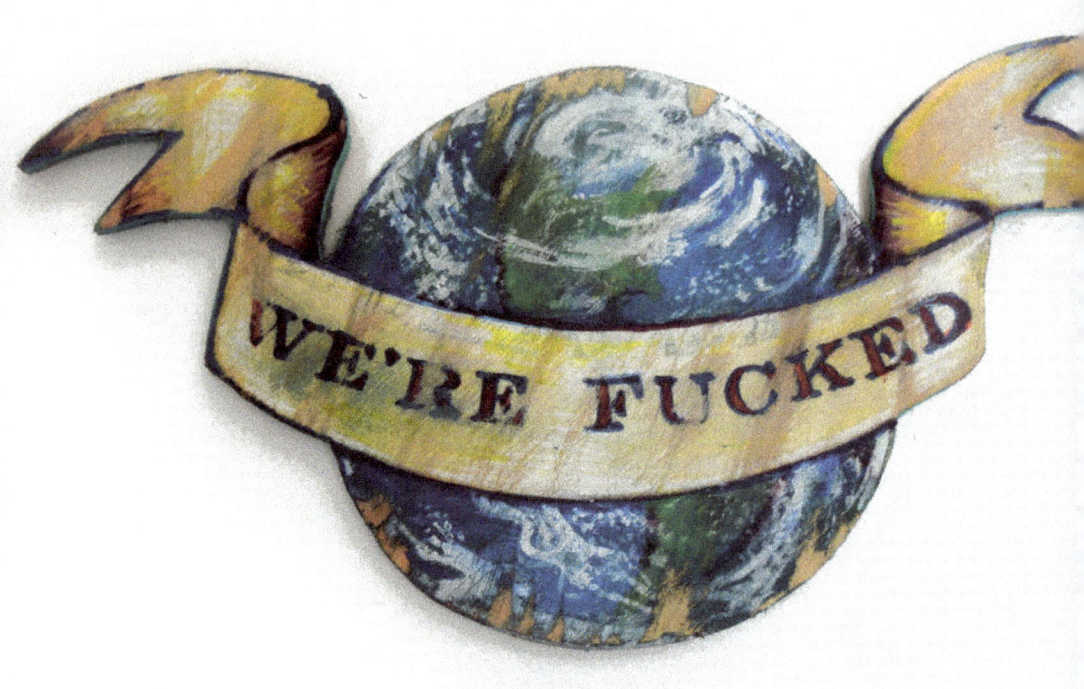

WE'RE
FUCKED

Would you go vegan if your life depended on it?

Few things in this world are better than grilled cheese. The way it gloops and melts and bubbles ;- mmm, utter deliciousness! I know this from past delicious experiences however because I'm now vegan. I don't eat cheese. Haven't eaten it or any other dairy products for almost ten years. But, I get it, when I first stopped eating it I'd still crave the salty, greasy loveliness that is grilled cheese on toast.

Before going vegan I ate cheese, lots of cheese, and before going vegetarian before that, I ate meat. Very few vegans are born vegan. When people ask me the thing I miss most now that I'm vegan, I'm usually whip-shot-quick at replying to them 'oh, mostly the guilt,' but if I'm honest, then yeah, there's a few salty greasy things I have delicious memories of.

However, if I said to you, you could save all life as we know it on this planet by just politely saying no to cheesy treats for the rest of your existence, would you do it?

Or if I said to you, you can live as you are now, with very little change, but without the looming catastrophic events currently threatening the environment and ecosystems around the planet, just by being a smidgeon more compassionate in your preferences, would you be open to it?

Also if I said to you that COVID19 was merely the first of a wave of killer Zoonotic diseases (such as Ebola, Sars and Rift Valley fever to name a few) that could easily wipe out all of humankind, but you could halt all of those oncoming viruses by simply altering your shopping and eating habits, would you even be bothered to consider it?

Because truth is, I'm afraid to say dear reader, these hypothetical questions are really, really quite real and not hypothetical at all.

Yup, I used to eat meat and dairy and then I realised, we actually have no time for that to be an option anymore.

Nine years ago my partner and I went vegan. Back then, the world seemed so much more a serene place and we believed we had time to not get too preachy, so gentle encouragement and passive education around all things plant-based was a casual hobby of mine. Live and let live seemed to be a wise philosophy.

I get it, people don't like self-righteous, preachy vegans.

Not everyone back then, knew about environmental issues or had a fair grasp that eating animals, at the scale we were/are, was unsustainable. Likewise, then, unlike now, certainly not everyone knew exactly what they could do to bring about change. But come on, now most people really do.

Certainly, where we are at now, in (as I write this) this almost post COVID 19 world, hesitancy or wilful ignorance around the environment is no longer a wise or fair option. It's a very selfish choice. Hell no. Get me a soapbox because sisters and brothers, now is the time to preach.

We are in the middle of a worldwide pandemic, environmental disaster is omnipresent, mass extinction seems pretty much inevitable. The number of zoonotic epidemics is on the rise. Here in Australia, most of us are scared shitless, bracing ourselves for extreme weather conditions such as the disastrous flooding we have recently seen in NSW, or on the horizon yet another extraordinarily drought-ridden hot summer dominated by inescapable firestorms.

A bit full-fucking-on isn't it! Don't like preachy vegans? Well, tough, you need to hear this!

I am thoroughly familiar with many reasons, well excuses really, as to why someone can't possibly go vegan "as much as they'd love to." Indulge me dear reader, as I run through some of those half-arsed call-and-responses.

"But I just crave dairy/cheese too much!" Yes, I know plant-based cheeses don't bubble the same when you grill them, but get used to it. Retrain your brain, ditch the dairy, lemmefuckintellya, oat milk in coffee is delicious! (once you get used to it)

"I just eat fish and white meat now, which is the more compassionate option!" For who exactly? Certainly not the millions of sea creatures killed through the trawling of the ocean or the millions of acres of sea floor left as dead zones. The oceans are dying, you are killing them. Also, DO NOT GET ME STARTED on the gruesome life of factory farmed chickens? White meat is still meat, a bird is still a sentient being.

'Oh, but I only eat organic/ethical/free range grass-fed beef!' This is completely unsustainable, do some research about massive forests being cleared and ecosystems destroyed for grazing pasture and then in turn what that does to weather cycles. The more room your organic cow has to move around the more damage it is doing. Also, wake-the-fuck-up, there's no such thing as ethical meet, no animal is ever slaughtered 'ethically', no animal wants to die.

'My doctor advised me against it!' Oh really, and did you seek out a second or third expert opinion or did you just nod and keep eating your pork pie like it was an apple?

There really is no excuse, or hiding place on this massively overpopulated planet, where you can pretend you don't know about the harm humankind is doing by its addiction to animal products. As a carnivore you only have one convincing argument and that is you simply don't give a shit about the future of all humankind. Own this because it's true.

To me, carnivore is definitely the worst C word in existence. Get yourself on the right side of history, there are many month-long campaigns out there, such as No Meat May, if you need encouragement and a structured focal point to ditch the dairy, give meat the chop and go plant based!

Don't just believe me, a while ago the utterly fucking fabulous, and way more distinguished Dr Jane Goodall summed it up best in an interview with the national Press Club. 'Masses of fossil fuel are used to get the grain to the animals, the animals to the abattoir, the meat to the table. Masses of water, which is in such short supply and drying in some areas, is used to get vegetable-to-animal protein. And, finally, they're all producing gas in their digestion and that's methane, and that is a very virulent greenhouse gas.'

Was she on her soapbox? Possibly. Does she have the right to be? Absofuckinglutely! Consider that pork pie bitch-slapped out of your hand by Dr Jane, now just exactly what kind of person would you be if you picked it up and kept eating?

Also, quite simply, you can't claim to be an animal lover and still fund factory farming. You know about the torture and killing of billions of farm animals annually, we all do. Wildlife population is being decimated around the world in countless diverse environments, driven by intensive agriculture and land clearance for livestock grazing (even just think about that soulless word 'livestock'). These acts are being done with your funding every time you buy some kind of animal or dairy products.

To me being vegan means being aware of the reality of where the world is at and wanting to be part of the solution rather than the ongoing, wilful ignorance causing the problem. We are all a work in progress, I started off being a carnivore, but I honestly couldn't justify it once I admitted to knowing the facts.

(To badly paraphrase the famous quote of 90s supermodel Kate Moss-) No toasted cheese tastes as good as living on a habitable planet feels.

So, are you going to go vegan? If not, what the ACTUAL FUCK do you need to be told to convince you? This isn't a wake-up call, it's a screeching fire alarm inside a burning house. Your house, where all of your family lives! And you are choosing to ignore it while you toast your cheese against the flames.

Salty, greasy loveliness should not cost us the earth, believe me, I'm an extremely experienced expert in this field, there are many plant-based types of junk food out there. Earlier in this piece I used the expression live and let live and I think that's a really interesting set of words to ponder on.

So, when I ask you, would you go vegan if your life depended on it? Quite simply; it does. All of our lives depend on it. It depends on you, now, today and because the very next mouthful you eat could be the global tipping point from which there is no return. Hate me if you want, but go vegan.

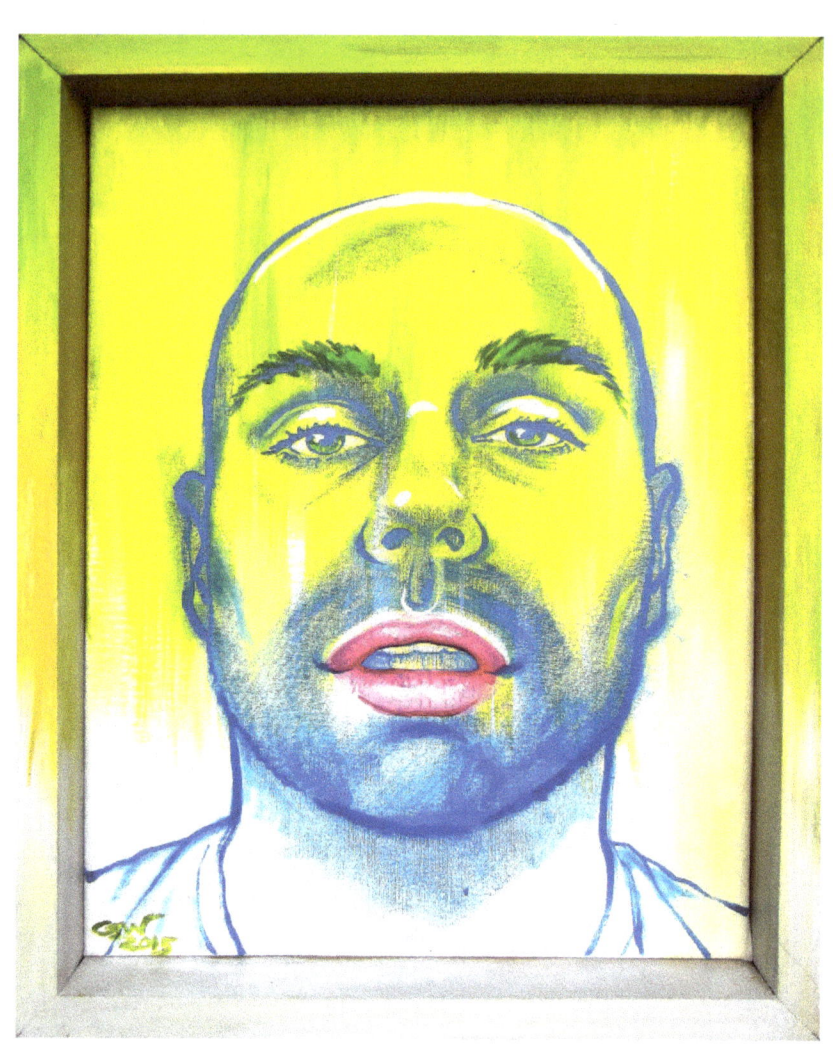

YELLOW ME

Yellow me needs to learn some things.

I found this painting in a pile of old work I'd put in a cupboard and forgotten about.

I tend to try and forget about works once they are done, especially self-portraits. There's not a lot to learn from them. They're done, they were possibly part of a process I needed to go through, so I move on! I did this one 5 years ago, I look at it and see a very unremarkable person staring back at me. Yellow has never been my colour. Truth be told, it's a bit of a dull painting, I like to think I wouldn't produce this painting now, five years can be hardly any time at all, or it can be a massive and important learning curve.

Not that I would really listen then (or sadly probably even now) but advice I would give to myself five years ago would be;-

Be braver, stop caring what people think about you. No one actually thinks about you, people only ever think about themselves anyway.

That book you want to write, make it happen and get a move on for fuck's sake! Stop waiting until things are desperately needing to be done.

Stop going out in the sun without sunscreen, the outcomes of that are SSOO gonna catch up with you.

Buy shares in something called Zoom.

Get a rescue dog, you're going to get a dog in four years' time anyway, but do it sooner unconditional love is fantastic and doggie cuddles keep you sane (ish).

Don't bother with that spell you go through of buying indoor plants, the fuckers only die and make you think that it's yet another thing you are shit at!

Don't allow a certain 'Mr X' to befriend you. You currently believe in his fabulousness, but it's a lie. Trust your gut feeling on this, anyone who sets your spider sense off, does so for a reason. Don't just allow them into your life because they seem cool and pursue your friendship. Your initial instincts are right, they are really not a good person, as you are about to find out.

Stop it already with the fear of aging thing. You're gonna age, there is no way to avoid it (well not without dying) embrace it because it's not gonna get either easier or prettier the more you deny it. Botox is not your lord and saviour, at best you just look like a middle aged man with a really reflective forehead.

In the next few years you'll learn an expression: 'there are two good times to plant a tree, 100 years ago, or today'. Think about what that really means. It means stop pissing about.

I'm asking the reader of this now to make a list of their own. What advice would you give yourself five years ago?

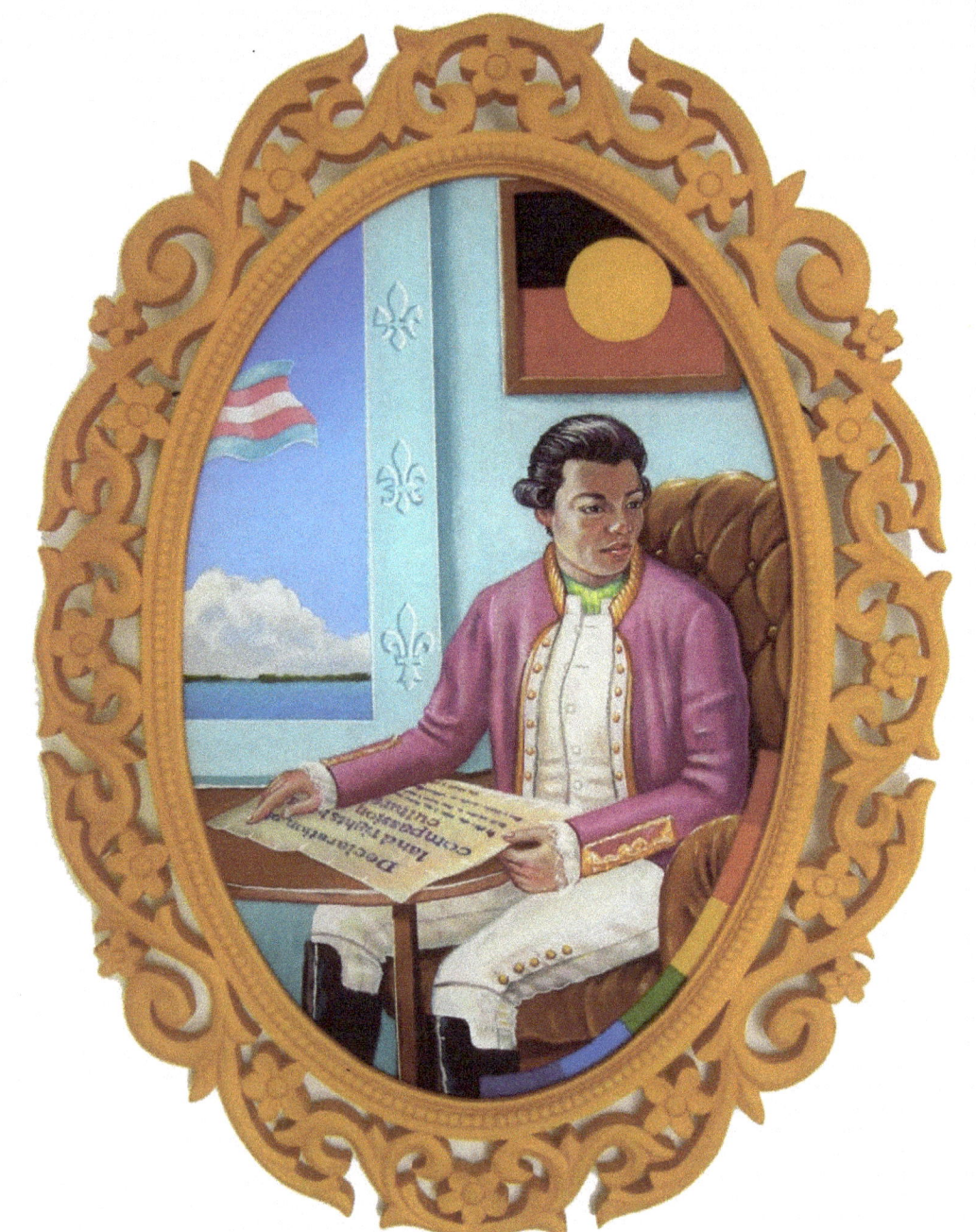

WHAT IF KINDER INTENTIONS HAD LED TO BETTER OUTCOMES?

Does this piece and its title speak for itself? I worry about all of this, about explaining what is behind my art and why I do what I do. What if I'm killing the 'magic' (not that I'm saying there's a lot of that to start with).

The model for this piece is my friend Xi, although it's kind of and mostly her, it's a rough likeness to say the least, I threw in some bits of my friend Marcia too for good measure. I kind of got a bit creative because I painted her during lockdown and it was done from a photo. It is meant to be a reference/fuck you to the famous painting of Captain Cook by Sir Nathaniel Dance-Holland as the so called 'discoverer' of Australia (don't fucking make me laugh, but more about that later) as he plots the East Coast.

This piece is about opening conversations around colonialism, how we can acknowledge what went so very wrong with the European invasion of Australia and what we can now do to right those (ongoing) wrongs.

What if Captain Cook had been a gender fluid or non-conforming, female bodied person of colour who was familiar with oppression and experienced in the importance of thinking with compassion rather than acting out of dominance and greed. What if Captain Cook just hadn't been such an absolute dick, knowing all along, he was above the law?

What if, what if?

This piece is about these possibilities, all possibilities and better possible results.

Just FYI, I wrote the above line down and then just stared at the words on the screen for about fifteen minutes, not sure what else to write, but with the word 'better possible results' flowing evocatively through my mind.

What could I have been if I'd been given a different start? What could any of us be if we had been offered a kinder, more encouraging beginning? It's a thought process worth having.

What if I hadn't only really started painting seriously in my thirties because I was too unsure of my own self-worth before that? What if I hadn't started writing and publishing work only now, as I enter my fifties, because as a child, I was repetitively told not to draw attention towards my own non-masculine voice. What if hundreds of thousands of indigenous people had not been slaughtered by the British invasion and the people of the First Nations still ruled in Australia with Europeans and other immigrants as welcome guests abiding by Indigenous laws and culture? What if a truthful history was taught in schools about how colonialism happened and that Australia was never 'discovered' by the British in 1770 (or indeed, the Dutch who originally named in 'New Holland' in 1606)? What if, when I first landed in Australia 22 years ago, I'd experience some kind of culture shock and had to learn a non-English language, or place names, foods and traditions? What if I didn't now live in an apartment block made up of almost entirely Caucasian residents on a land mass so very close to Asia? What if, instead of the government funding a chaplain, teaching a Christian belief system in every school in Australia, they funded a person of First Nation heritage to lead discussions around traditional ceremonies and ways of being (and being more connected to the environment)?

So much in my work invokes and suggests 'what if's' and that is something I like about it. Yes, I struggle with painting hands, capturing likenesses from photos and I may not be the most accomplished of painters, but I started late and never actually studied art, however, what if things had been different there?

What if I hadn't had a father that just had no idea how to parent a queer child?

What if at school I'd been encouraged to explore the queer-er side of my personality rather than being shamefully forced into trying to hide it beneath something very similar to self-loathing?

What if I hadn't been told to not speak unless I could make myself sound like a man, but encouraged to consider what I, and others who shared my oppression, had to say?

What if I, at aged 10, hadn't had a Physical education teacher throw a football into my chest as hard as he possibly could, and when I fell back winded, laugh and proudly proclaim 'I'm not surprised your father hates you!' in order to make himself popular with the sport loving bullies in my class?

What if I wasn't constantly, overwhelmingly afraid of the doorbell ringing when I was in our family home because if it woke up our dozing father he would probably go on a violent rampage?

What if, as a teenager I hadn't been the school punching bag?

What if I hadn't thought that every man I dated in my twenties and thirties was too good for me and I was doing them a favour by setting them free?

What if I'd thrown that ball back at Mr Woods in Physical education and screamed, 'It's not up to you to tell me about my father.'?

What if Donald Trump's father had worn a condom?

What if, if we did get bitten by radioactive spiders, as I'd hoped for as a child, we did get fabulous superpowers (instead of, lets presume; cancer)?

What if I could rock a tie, waistcoat and skinny jeans without looking like The Penguin from Batman?

What if I didn't just try to cover up a moment, every time it got too real, with humour so people would still like me and not think me too intense? I may need to work on that.

What if, what if, what if.

What if kinder intentions had led to better outcomes?

www.ingramcontent.com/pod-product-compliance
Lightning Source LLC
Chambersburg PA
CBHW040953170526
45159CB00014B/3122